ISLAND

THROUGH THE YEARS

This Island by herself exists
A separate thing. Alone she lies,
Cut from the main.
Held in the sea's embrace, she resists
That violence and the sky's
Outbursts — the tempest black, the hurricane.

Always some threat, some peril, persists.
The Island with hauteur defies.
Through freeze and fire and years of pain
Her spirit holds and holds. It never dies.

This oasis that we well know
And love a living creature is, one who
Delights to please, to shelter and to serve.
Strong though she is, she is also
A species rare, endangered, one of few
In this rude world. Her charms deserve
From us who come and go
Vigilance, devotion. These are her due.
And friendship that will not fail or swerve.

To our Island home, this pledge:
Fidelity unfailing, and love and care.
Enchantress by the deep sea's edge,
When you need us, we'll be there.

H.L.

Byway to a Special World

To enter the long canopy of ficus trees and pass under their filtered sunlight is, to borrow a phrase from Charles Dickens, to leave behind a universe as "mad as bedlam" and enter a haven of quiet, companionable life. No condominium towers thrust up to spoil an expanse of sky, a cobalt sea, or dawn light spreading silver tracery over the breaking surf. Jupiter Island's beauty is a balance between nature and man's artful adaptations that enhance but do not overpower the original. These ficus trees were saplings when they were planted by Permelia Reed in 1940. Now they are as much a part of the Island as the casuarinas. Hibiscus greets us everywhere. Stroll across a painted bridge to find a tiny isle lovely in wilderness and blessed with orchid trees. Look west, past oleanders and rustling palms, and see the sparkling river, the dock and the boats lazing in the sun. Beauty here is a simple fact of life.

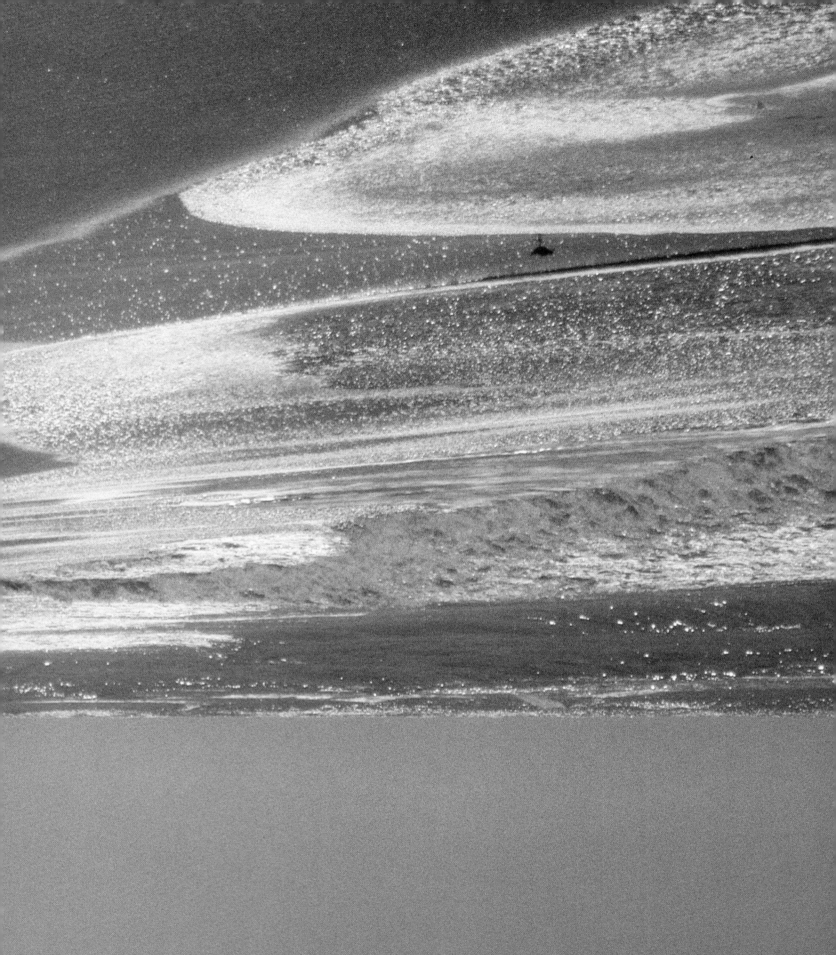

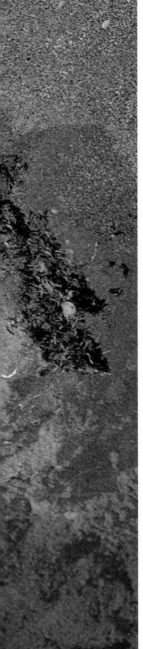

Manatee, descendant of the prehistoric elephant, uses its prehensile feet grazing in the flats of the Hobe Sound estuary where more than 250 of them pass the winters. It frequently exceeds eight ft. in length, 600 lbs. in weight. Its protection and fate rest in the hands of caring man.

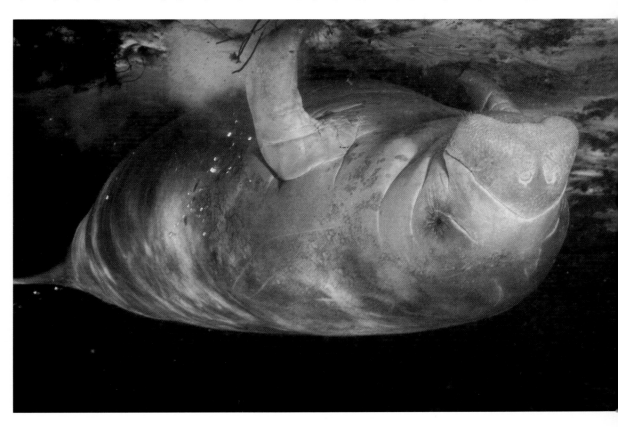

The Precious Wild World

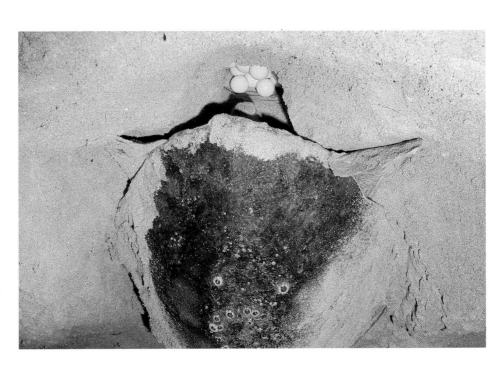

A 225 lb. loggerhead (above) nests with single-minded purpose, oblivious to any disturbance. Upper left, another nesting loggerhead is seen from the rear, her eggs accumulating beneath her. She will lay 112 eggs the size of ping pong balls and then, like the 250 lb. green turtle at left, return to the sea. Total nesting process takes an hour. Eggs hatch in 55 days. Below, baby loggerheads, having emerged from the nest 18 inches deep in sand, scurry to the surf. They are 1.25 in. long, will be full-grown in 15-20 years.

by Nathaniel Reed

J upiter Island is but a geological child, the whimsical creation of the sea-level of the Pleistocene Era. When the rolling scrub pine hills of Jonathan Dickinson Park were sea dunes, Jupiter Island was but a sandbar. The Island's backbone is Anastasia limestone, a seemingly random accretion and a solidification of minute sea particles. The limestone rock is concealed beneath a mantle of golden sands, as shifting and unpredictable today as when they arrived. Atop this dynamic, now elevated, relic sandbar are found a unique assemblage of plant communities. These range from Florida's northernmost tropical hammocks growing on the highest elevations, down through the salt-tolerant strand community, to the beach species which inhabit the shifting dunes. Along the Hobe Sound estuary are found excellent examples of the mangrove community. These are the land-builders; plants forever attempting to lay claim to shallow, calm waters with tenacious finger-like roots.

Mangrove builds the land. Its constantly dropping leaves form a rich, organic, underwater blanket which Fall and Spring high tides wash into the lagoon. There the detritus fertilizes the grass beds, and it is the major force stimulating the great spectrum of aquatic life.

Skimming low, a Blue Heron (left) commences its elegant ascent. Above, a Brown Pelican preens himself. An ultimate predator, he feasts on minnows and mullet; is noted for his plummeting dives.

Distinctively sculpted by centuries of climatic and edaphic influence, the biotic community of Jupiter Island is still continually reshaped even by the annual season.

Fall brings the first north winds, bearing both visitors and residents to Jupiter Island. As the Main Club is opened and grounds dressed, myriads of warblers dart past en route to South America. The Golf House opens, and owls arrive to take up residence in the adjacent tall Australian pine trees. Early morning golfers find flights of blue-wing teal and other waterfowl resting amid the resident birds on the golf course ponds. Errant golfers may find tracks of nocturnal foxes and bobcats in traps and bunkers. Luncheon visitors to the Beach Club may see the annual migrations of bluefish and spanish mackerel pursuing baitfish schools in the surf line.

Jupiter Island's most distinctive winter visitors are rarely seen by those who inhabit Jupiter Island. They arrive singly, or sometimes in small groups. They arrive at all hours, and stay for varying times depending upon weather and inclination. They arrive quietly and truly with hardly a ripple, for

"they" are the manatees which return each year to the grass pastures of the Hobe Sound estuary. Air-breathing aquatic mammals, the manatees are exceedingly vulnerable from collisions with high speed boats, and the waters of Hobe Sound have special speed restrictions to protect the winter population. Only about 1000 remain in Florida; as much as 20% of the entire population has been seen feeding in Hobe Sound on a single winter morning. During cooler periods, the manatees move south to Riviera Beach and Lake Worth to bask in the warm water discharge created by the FP & L electric power generating plant. As temperatures climb following passage of a winter front, the animals return to the feeding areas in Hobe Sound. Much of their time is spent basking in shallow water and manatees often are seen behind Harbor Island, around the Club Dock, and along the 13th fairway.

With warming conditions in the Spring, these manatees disperse back northward along the Florida coast, and move upstream in Florida rivers to consume other forms of aquatic vegetation. While manatees are seen in Hobe Sound throughout

On this page are four imported plants that flourish on the Island: Ginger Lily (left), Bottlebrush (top), the Passion Flower (center), and, of course, Bougainvillea. At right is a native, the Yucca, lovely and tender in its bloom, but tough. Rooted well in the sandy soil, it is impervious to direct salt spray.

the year, summer sightings are much less common.

Jupiter Island's winter residents typically depart as spring arrives. The rainy season commences, and the Island vegetation dons summer dress; temperate winter browns are replaced by sub-tropical summer greens. Native plants, having spent the winter upstaged by more colorful exotic landscape plantings, burst forth with their own distinctive displays. No plant more dramatically heralds the coming of summer than the stalwart Yucca. Tenaciously perched atop the dunes, they greet the morning sun adorned with a brilliant white inflorescent spire. In May's moon they stand as shimmering sentinels, seemingly nature's guidebeacons for wandering seafarers.

With summer, seafarers do indeed return to Jupiter Island. They've been at sea for at least two or three years, some much longer, and they've ranged all the Atlantic coast, the Northern Caribbean, and the Gulf of Mexico. Consummate navigators, they found land 200 million years before Columbus, and remain our earliest successful colonists. These seafarers are the sea turtles, returning each summer to nest on the beaches of Jupiter Island. Four different species, including leatherback turtles weighing over one thousand pounds, visit each summer. Most of the turtles are smaller loggerheads, apparently so named for both appearance and disposition. Crawling ashore under the cover of darkness, each female conceals about 100 eggs in a carefully excavated chamber. The entire nesting effort requires an hour, and may be repeated several times at two-week intervals. Early July finds Jupiter Island a maze of tracks and nest pits; by August, more than 3500 nests will have been hidden in the warm sands. If not discovered by foraging raccoons or claimed by storm seas, the eggs will incubate for almost 60 days before the baby turtles emerge. These hatchlings first, and last, communal act will be to emerge together from the nest cavity and scuttle to the sea. After an essentially nomadic solitary, aquatic life for perhaps 15-20 years, the mature females may return to a Pleistocene sandbar, framed in Yucca blooms to continue one of the unique cycles of Jupiter Island.

A Veritable Cafeteria of Fish

by Tom Stanley

An abundance of game fish in the waters surrounding Jupiter Island served as a magnet in the late 1800s, attracting sport fishermen from far and near. In those early days it took real dedication to get to the Island. Before the coming of Flagler's railroad in the 1890s, access from the outside world was limited to paddle wheel steamers or sailing craft.

Snook, tarpon, speckled trout, channel bass (redfish), mangrove snapper, jack crevalle and ladyfish were plentiful and desired as game species. Bottom dwellers such as sheepshead, drum, croaker and sand perch provided entertainment for children and delectable table fare. Offshore fishing for pelagic species such as sailfish, dolphin (fish), wahoo and king mackerel was not discovered until after the turn of the century when gasoline-powered boats made it possible to venture into the sometimes turbulent Gulfstream.

The estuary and ecosystem at the turn of the century was very different from the one we have today. The Intracoastal Waterway did not exist. The Indian River terminated at Jupiter and boats could not make inside passage to Lake Worth and Palm Beach. Freight and passengers headed for places south of Jupiter were loaded aboard the Celestial Railway, a short-haul line which connected at Juno, on the north end of Lake Worth, with other boats bound for Miami and points between. Dredging of the straight channels north of Bridge Road occurred after 1910, altering the typical "S" curves of a coastal tidal waterway, and thus the Saint Lucie Inlet carried a fraction of today's flow. The inlet at Jupiter was open only on a seasonal basis. Prevailing southeast winds of spring and summer shifted the beach sand, which had been carried off shore by fall and winter storms, back to shore. This process blocked the flow during some of the summer months — a story familiar to those now paying an erosion tax. It is documented that the Barefoot Mailman who delivered mail on foot down the East Coast walked across the sand beach at the site of the present Inlet. The water impounded by this sand barrier included the entire drainage basin of the Loxahatchee River.

Tidal movement of the Indian River at Hobe Sound was impeded; this created a body of salt and brackish water with little current, an area consisting largely of red mangrove flats. A more perfect incubator for fish would be hard to devise. Fallen red mangrove leaves quickly decay; this begins the food chain which nourishes newly incubated young of virtually every marine species.

Nature timed this sequence of events to perfection. Torrential rainfall in the hurricane season caused waters of the Loxahatchee to rise and the resulting pressure forced first a trickle and then a torrent through the temporary dam at the mouth of the Inlet. Fingerlings of every variety were snatched from the sanctuary of their hatchery and thrust into the mainstream to serve as prey for the game fish which congregated to feed inside the Inlet. All this, plus the restoration of tidal cycles, created a veritable cafeteria of fish which were served twice daily to waiting anglers.

The first four decades of this century provided some of the finest inshore fishing on this planet. Clear, clean water flowed over brilliant white sand the full length of Jupiter in both river and ocean. Aquatic life was varied and abundant. Oysters from large beds in the Loxahatchee — about where the present railroad bridge crosses — and from a smaller bed in Peck's Lake on the north end were succulent fare. Clams were there for the taking, and conch were present until the mid-twenties. Grass beds were home for exotic species of tropical fish. Game fish continued to be plentiful and fishing pressure made no noticeable dent in their numbers.

In the late twenties a disaster occurred. At the time there was no apparent connection with the great fishing in these waters, but it marked the beginning of the end. In September 1928, a hurricane swept across the Florida peninsula, concentrating its fury on Lake Okeechobee. Water from the lake was literally blown out to engulf surrounding communities of Clewiston, Belle Glade and other nearby settlements at its southern end. More than 2,000 inhabitants who had no high ground for refuge were trapped by the flood and drowned. A horrified nation reacted at once. A massive dike was planned. Completely encircling the Lake, this barrier would divert its normal southerly flow and carry it through man-made canals to the east, spilling into the Atlantic.

This achievement — the Okeechobee Flood Control Project — unwittingly destroyed the estuary between the Saint Lucie and Loxahatchee Rivers, as well as that of much of the lower Everglades. Massive quantities of silt-laden fresh water poured down the Saint Lucie Canal and through the Loxahatchee slough. This lowered salinity and effectively poisoned the salt and brackish water hatchery which for millenia had nurtured and nourished a teeming population of fish of all kinds. White sand river shores and bottoms were covered with a choking layer of silt and mud, killing most grass beds. This instantly sent tropical species fleeing to cleaner ocean waters. Other bottom-feeders followed when accumulation passed their level of tolerance and the river was left with mostly coarse fish.

In time this blanket of mud and silt reached the shallow reefs near Jupiter Island beaches and reduced or eliminatd most species there, including snapper and grouper, two of the most sought after food fish. The Everglades, deprived of its normal flow of life-giving fresh water, became too saline at its southern extremities to incubate many important species. It became too dry along its "river of grass" mid-section to initiate the food chain that had nourished the entire southern estuary of the Florida peninsula. The inevitable decline of all forms of marine life was thus assured. Modern "development," accompanied by bulkheading, drainage ditches, quick runoff and pollution caused by increased population exacerbated the problem. (It is encouraging to observe that the South Florida Water Management District, recognizing a need to restore some of this lost resource, is searching for solutions to the problem.)

While fishing was an activity enjoyed by many Island residents in the 1920s, perhaps none pursued it with such fervor as the Bassett, Stanley and Vaughan families. They could be found most weekday afternoons (following morning golf) coursing Indian River waters in pursuit of finned quarry. The vessels used were 18-foot cedar-strip Penn Yan boats powered by Johnson Seahorse outboard motors. Ten horsepower was top of the line, and mininaturization had not then occurred. It took two able-bodied men to lift one of these monsters.

These craft were soon replaced by small inboard cabin boats based in Bassett Creek at docks constructed with permission of the Hobe Sound Company. In a conclave of five households it was natural that a spirit of competition emerged. Chauffeurs at each house doubled as boat captains, and wagers between rivals were not uncommon — stakes never being revealed to the boss. All-day trips were reserved for Saturday to accommodate children of school age. Sumptuous lunches were carefully stowed, and the flotilla would embark for Peck's Lake, Jupiter or some other "distant" destination. Success was virtually assured as it was almost impossible not to catch more fish than was needed for home consumption. These catches were never wasted. Boat captains distributed the excess to friends in Gomez and Banner Lake. The Okeechobee Flood Control Project spoiled much of the fishing in the area, but it did not get all of the blame. The story goes that two natives were overheard talking in front of St. Onge's Grocery in Hobe Sound. The conversation went something like this.

"Been fishin' lately?"

"Yeah."

"Catch anything?"

"Naw, 'dem Bassetts done caught 'em all!"

The rate of success in surf fishing is greater now than in early years. This is the result of improvement in fishing tackle. The skills required to cast a six ounce lead sinker and terminal tackle with a single action reel, filled with waxed linen line, mounted on a calcutta rod weighing about 15 pounds were too difficult for most people to master. Only experts could cast far enough to reach many fish, and even they experienced frequent backlashes that were hard to untangle. Now that spinning reels and monofilament make it easier to cast, skilled anglers can catch fish previously out of reach. In the early days the area around Blowing Rocks was one of the most popular fishing spots. Pompano could be found there in quantity more often than not. Bluefish, when in season, as well as croaker and whiting were mainstays. Bluefish, accompanied by flocks of dipping, diving, screaming seagulls, usually moved up or down the beach when feeding on schools of baitfish. There was unlimited access to the beach in those days, and an enterprising surf fisherman would play leapfrog with the school, gathering his gear and driving to a good vantage point to await their arrival. Often, in the interest of time, he would quickly bury his catch for later retrieval and then move to intercept the "blues" farther along the beach. This precaution was necessary, not because of fear that fellow anglers would abscond with the catch, but because of the flocks of hungry gulls.

Offshore fishing, today, is better than ever, thanks to improved tackle and to conservation measures which seem to be preserving sailfish for future generations. Most sailfish which are brought to the boat are released to fight again. More boats sail each day, and more sailfish are caught now than 50 or even 30 years ago. But the supply seems stable. In February 1986, three Palm Beach-based sportfishing boats caught and released 72 sailfish in a span of five hours five miles east of the Jupiter Island Beach Club. Blue and white marlin, almost never seen in years past, have become more common in the 1980s. Blue marlin tournaments now are held annually in Palm Beach and Fort Lauderdale; and white marlin migrate through these waters in April.

Unfortunately, other desired species including spanish mackerel, king mackerel, dolphin, wahoo, amberjack and grouper have not fared as well. Fishing pressure, both commercial and recreational, has severely depleted the supply of spanish and king mackerel, and grave questions exist as to their chances for survival. Roller net boats directed to schools by spotter planes are just too effective, and breeding stocks have been mortally damaged. Other species mentioned are becoming scarce.

Many Island residents have enjoyed offshore fishing. One of the earlier active sportsmen was Burr Bartram who maintained lovely boats here. A number of residents were longtime clients of two unique fishing operations. Captain Ad Whiticar moved to Stuart from New Jersey in 1917 as a commercial fisherman. He later started the Whiticar Sports Fishing Fleet using boats built by his son at Whiticar Boat Works. Toley Engebretsen founded Toley's Boatyard and later branched out into charter fishing. They were largely responsible for establishing Stuart as "Sailfish Capital of the World."

Toley, as a young man in his native Sweden, built a sailboat and loaded his wife and children aboard bound for the new world. A master boat builder, craftsman and jack-of-all-trades, known simply as "Dad," accompanied him. One of their first commissions was the ANN B. II, built for Governor and Mrs. Stanley in 1935. Whiticar Boat Works continues in operation under management by descendants of Captain Ad, and at least one island resident, Bronson Ingram, sails the waters in his magnificent Whiticar sportfishing yacht, the *Patsea,* which graces the Club dock for a part of each season. John Richmond, Hugo Rutherfurd, Nathaniel Reed, John and George Vaughan and others can frequently be found seeking sport in Gulfstream waters, and I join them there in the "Chinese Fire Drill."

Fishing tournaments conducted by the Club for youngsters a decade or two ago are among their fondest memories. Who can forget the thrill of receiving a trophy for "Longest Puffer" or "Smallest Snapper?" Perhaps it's time to resurrect this source of enjoyment. John D. and Pocahontas Bassett, who lived a combined total of 188 healthy and active years, surely attest to truth as well as poetry in the proverb which declares: "Allah does not take from man's allotted time on earth those hours spent fishing."

The author posed with a day's catch in 1935 when the fishing was great. "At that age," he says, "it was easy to be 'out-counted' by elders so I kept my fish on a string as a precaution."

Exploring the Past

by Hobart Lewis

At the southern tip of Jupiter Island the lighthouse stands like a sentinel. It is not only a guide and protector of ships, but a landmark, a symbol of the Island itself. Built in 1859, it was designed by Lt. George G. Meade, who later became the Federal Commander at Gettysburg. It was first lighted on July 10, 1860, but during the Civil War southern patriots darkened it to allow blockade runners to enter the Inlet unobserved. It was relighted on June 28, 1866 and has been a beacon for shipping ever since. It is also an excellent place from which to view the area. A visitor who was cruising the Florida coast in 1884 describes the scene:

"From Conch Bar we saw the tall brick tower of Jupiter Light which we reached during the afternoon. It is a first-class, revolving light, made in France, and shows a succession of flashes, followed by a somewhat prolonged, steady light. The tower, one hundred feet high, stands on a bluff fifty feet above the water — at the confluence of Indian and Loxahatchee Rivers, where they unite and flow as Jupiter River for a mile eastward and over Jupiter Bar into the sea. From the balcony surrounding the lantern the view is at once grand and comprehensive.

"First we see Indian River stretching away for miles toward the north where, in the distance, we obtain but fugitive glances of it between the intervening hills and clumps of foliage, 'like orient pearls at random strung.' Then the Loxahatchee winding along through the savannas with many a devious turn, like a huge serpent gliding from the setting sun toward the sea. Toward the south lies a panorama of pines, cypresses, and saw-grass, with varying tints of green amidst which is a network of small streams glinting in the sunlight like a filigree of silver; while far beyond lies Lake Worth, a burnished shield on a velvet sword. Turning at last toward the east we behold grand old ocean, 'dark, deeply beautiful blue,' stretching away to the vast horizon where the blue above meets the blue below.

"South-southeastward of Stuart for fifteen miles, the eastern bank of the Indian River is formed by Jupiter Island which, at most places, is considerably less than one mile in width."

In the early days the only approach to Jupiter Island was by boat. It is still an excellent way to explore it. Climb aboard.

We enter the Inlet at the lighthouse and bear north, up the Intracoastal. On the east, the first sight is a line of high-rise condominiums, stark and white, blotting out all view of the sea and, almost, of the sky. Flanking the west bank is a busy highway, U.S. 1, with its traffic and its clutter of marinas, motels and gas stations. All of them are necessary but none of them planned to please the eye or the residents of Jupiter Island proper, who are very proper indeed.

Back To Nature

Suddenly, you are aware that something has happened to the surroundings, something that changes the view — both East and West. What has happened is that foresight and planning have prevailed — no more condominiums, no more highway helter-skelter. Instead, the east shore is, literally, a landscape architect's dream. For mile after mile well-behaved lawns and well-dressed gardens incline from well-mannered houses to the "River." And across the River there is a glimpse of what Florida was "before white man came."

For some three miles the western shore of the Waterway is lined with lush tropical vegetation — sea grape, mangrove, palm trees, palmetto. This pristine jungle is home to colonies of crane, heron, ibis and egrets — birds whose families have vacationed here for thousands of years, a very pretty picture, an exercise in primeval loveliness.

The picture today would be very different if Jupiter Islanders had not looked ahead. Instead of wilderness there would be a different jungle — one infested with the dangerous beasts of traffic. Lynxes, Cougars and Jaguars would be roaring night and day. Instead of Great Blue Herons, flocks of Thunderbirds, Firebirds and Falcons would be seen flying down to Miami.

All this and much more would have occurred if foresight had not intervened. Fortunately, the principal owners of the Island took action. Together with a group of friends they purchased this stretch of wilderness. It is now protected by the Fish and Wildlife Service, and remains unspoiled, shielded from highway and high-rises alike.

So, wilderness on the West, the Atlantic Ocean on the East. What about the North and what about the South? Have no fear. At the south end of the residential part of the Island a tract of wild land was bought and given to The Nature Conservancy. This tract, which would have been a modern developer's delight (i.e. blight) is, instead, Blowing Rocks Preserve, forever wild. It is a glorious place to watch the sea waves thrash against the coast, a place Winslow Homer would have loved. At the north end, too, the door has been closed — and locked. Here, a large stretch of wilderness was given to the Hobe Sound National Wildlife Refuge, completing the circle, and making Jupiter Island truly an island, surrounded by a sea of nature, untouched — and untouchable — by man or bulldozer.

Very well, but what *is* Jupiter Island? In truth, it is a way of life — a community that is rather determinedly old-fashioned. Here is a small winter colony that was founded more than fifty years ago, that is very conscious of its traditions, fond of its eccentricities and unwilling to believe that Palm Beach, for example, or for an even worse example, Miami, have all the answers or, indeed, have any answers at all.

In the beginning the Island was home to the Indians, the Seminoles, and to alligators, manatees, rattlesnakes, raccoons, panthers, wild pigs and the like. The greatest natural influence on the area — then and now — has been the Gulf Stream. It is the Gulf Stream that makes Florida what it is, a benign (usually) and comfortable home for man and beast. As such, the Gulf Stream deserves a brief introduction.

Dark Blue River In The Sea

It is not too much to say that the Gulf Stream is the engine which by its constant heat and energy makes Florida what Ponce de Leon found it to be and so named it — *The Land of Flowers*. To be sure, the latitude helps. It is in the temperate zone — on a line with Egypt — but the warmth of the Gulf Stream passing near its eastern shore is what brings out the bikinis in January.

This mighty ocean river is not merely a single phenomenon but is part of a vast and complex system of ocean currents that circle up and down and across the Atlantic Ocean. Initially, the Gulf Stream flows west from Africa, driven by the Trade Winds. It enters the Gulf of Mexico, courses around it, and emerges through the Florida Straits. From here it flows North-Northeast and warms the eastern United States. Off the coast of New England it divides. One current heads toward Newfoundland, the other flows toward the British Isles, causing palm trees to grow in Ireland and lemon trees to bear fruit in Devonshire.

And how does this natural wonder affect Jupiter Island? Immensely. For here the Stream comes very close to the mainland. From the Jupiter Island Beach Club the great dark blue river in the sea is only four miles away. On a clear day it can be clearly seen. It flows from South to North at some four miles an hour, turning winter into summer as it goes.

Seminoles, Spaniards And Speculators

The Seminoles played a considerable role in Florida for many years and were to occupy the attention of the U.S. Government for many more. From 1835 to 1848 the U.S. Army waged war against them. Their effective presence ended when most of the Seminoles were removed to the Oklahoma Territory. (The less said about *that* the better!)

The first visitors to Jupiter Island were the Spanish who in their great period of exploration discovered "the new world." In 1492, Christopher Columbus claimed all that he found in the name of Ferdinand and Isabella, King and Queen of Spain. In 1513, Ponce de Leon landed on the peninsula. In 1565, St. Augustine was founded — the oldest city in the U.S.

For the next 200 years Florida was a pawn in a chess game played by three empire builders — Spain, France and England. After 1782, America entered the game and gradually picked up the pieces. (Florida did not become a U.S. possession until 1821.) Just before that, in 1815, Jupiter Island and some 12,000 acres around it were bestowed by the King and Queen of Spain on one Eusebio Gomez. This was a Royal Grant, a kind of tip for "services rendered."

After this grant, the story becomes the familiar undulating cycle of Florida real estate deals. The undulations are like greens on a golf course. You never know which way — or when — the ball is going to roll.

The ball began to roll in 1821 when Florida became a U.S. possession. In that year Eusebio Gomez sold three quarters of his royal grant, some 8000 acres. This parcel became the property of an American, one Joseph Delespine. The price was $8,000. The next year Delespine sold 4000 of his acres to a Michael Lazarus for $4000. This Lazarus must have known something his predecessors did not know. For two years later he sold his 4000 acres (plus a few improvements) for $50,000 — clear profit. (No income tax, no capital gains tax!)

So much for the 8000 acres Senor Gomez sold. What happened to the 4000 acres still left in the Gomez Grant? What happened is more or less the "modern" history of Jupiter Island.

These 4000 acres included Jupiter Island, and they remained unwanted — or at least unsold — for 71 years, until 1892. Then things began to boil.

Of Fortunes And Frozen Assets

In that year a group of Englishmen, younger sons of younger sons and hence "remittance men," came to the new world to seek their fortune. Many adventurers were, of course, attracted to the new United States in those new days. Some came seeking gold, some were slave traders, others sought cheap land for investment. The group that concerns us was somewhat original. They were looking for land on which to grow pineapples. They found it on Jupiter Island and on the mainland across the Indian River — the remaining 4000 acres of the Gomez Grant. (The Englishmen built a little railroad on the Island to transport their pineapples. It ran along what is now Links Road to the dock, and went South beyond the Gomez-Beach Road fork in the road.)

As has happened since in Florida real estate, the land, once it was purchased, became attractive to other investors. Another group of Englishmen, from Yorkshire this time, were exploring the U.S. for good land prospects. They invested heavily in Texas. And in Florida they bought large tracts of land — $2,500,000 worth. In their travels these Yorkshiremen came upon Jupiter Island and, as so many visitors since have, fell in love with it. Their response was immediate and direct. They formed the Indian River Association, Ltd., bought the former Gomez Grant from the pineapple growers, left these men to remain as "tenant farmers," and returned to England. There, they waited to see which way the ball was going to roll.

They didn't have long to wait. They were aiming high, but the ball rolled the other way — downhill and into the rough. And it was really rough! In 1895 the Big Freeze came — one of those disasters that, Gulf Stream or no Gulf Stream, occasionally turns the Land of Flowers into the land of icicles. The citrus crop was finished. Oranges, lemons, grapefruit turned black and hard as rocks. All other crops, including the pineapple, were killed. Overnight, the state was ruined, and so were the British who had invested in the land of frozen flowers.

When word of the freeze reached England a chill went through the Land Mortgage Bank of Yorkshire. The bonds of the English company were now $1 million in arrears. The bank shivered for a few days and then made a wise move. It sent to Jupiter Island one William Angas to represent the investors and to try to warm things up again.

The Man Who Came To Stay

William Angas must have been a very canny and very sturdy Scot. He sailed out at once, settled in Jacksonville, and went down to the Island to survey the ruins. He then agreed to stay on for five years to see if he could recoup. He made some progress and at the end of five years agreed to carry on for five more.

By 1905 it was "mission accomplished"; ten years after the freeze Angas managed to repay all of the principal, if not the interest, on the Yorkshire bonds. He had liquidated all of the English investment in Florida — except the Hobe Sound Company. He might then have returned home to a hero's welcome. Instead, he moved himself and his family to Jupiter Island. He was still the representative of the Land Mortgage Bank of Yorkshire and the operating head of the Hobe Sound Company. His mission now was to develop the property — the Island and some acreage on the mainland. It was a job that would have daunted anyone but William Angas.

In 1905, only twelve white families lived on the Island and in the town of Hobe Sound across from it. There was no bridge to the Island. All access and travel between the few houses and fishing camps was by boat. There were no roads and no doctor for ninety miles. (In case of death the women tended the body while the men dug the grave.) The natives were friendly but the snakes and the mosquitoes were not. In spite of the efforts to discourage him, William Angas stayed on.

He cut away the mangroves and built retaining walls along the river. He dug drainage ditches, cleared swamps, put in paths and roads, and he built a golf course. Angas seemed always to have in mind a resort hotel which would attract visitors to Jupiter Island. In 1911 an event occurred which gave him hope. In that year the north bridge across the waterway was opened and a road was brought part way down the Island. Mr. Angas decided now was the time to build.

On behalf of the English Company he borrowed $12,000 from Lucius Robinson (the father of Mrs. Fred Gordon) and put up a small hotel and three cottages. This was the birth of Jupiter Island as a winter colony. It is notable that the exterior and layout of the present main clubhouse and the cottages, *Alamanda* and *Bamboo*, are the same today as they were when the hotel opened. This was in 1916. The hotel was called *The Island Inn*.

High Hopes

The venture was so successful that within two years the English company was able to repay the original investment. During the next four years Mr. Angas built more cottages, enlarged the Inn's lounge, the kitchen and improved the golf course. He seemed to have been a man with expansive — and expensive — ideas. He wanted to put still more into the Jupiter Island "experiment." Times had changed back home, however, and the idea didn't play well in Yorkshire. World War I had just ended, everyone was weary — and understandably bearish. The English owners, now the second and third generations of the original investors, decided they had had enough. They instructed Mr. Angas to sell their holdings. Their timing was perfect. The railroad had pushed all the way to Key West. The first Florida boom was going strong. In 1923 William Angas sold out to something called the Olympia Improvement Corporation.

They must have been a high-powered bunch, these Olympia people. They had an eye-popping blueprint for Jupiter

1916. Top: Beginning to build The Island Inn, now the Main Club. Center: The Tangerine Theatre — host to movies, lectures, meetings, concerts, etc. — was built on this site. Above: Mariner Cottage — one of several original cottages — home to guests for almost 70 years.

Island, surveyed and drawn by Carr and McFadden, Inc., Civil Engineers of West Palm Beach, dated 1925. From the Gomez-Beach Road fork to Bridge Road the ocean and river fronts are ringed with 100 foot-wide lots, one packed against the other. The land within this dense perimeter, except for the nine hole golf course, is organized into similar lots. This is called Olympia Beach. But on North Beach Road, with Gomez extending north and parallel to it, appears another massive housing complex with the same narrow lots crowded into the white-lined network on the blueprint paper. This is entitled "Bon Air Beach, " and North Beach Road is enobled with a grand old name, "Royal Palm Boulevard". On the mainland, Olympia planned a Grecian-style town adjacent to a Florida Hollywood called Picture City. The moguls and stars of the screen would work on the mainland and live in splendor along Royal Palm Boulevard in multi-lot mansions overlooking the great ocean.

Sell-Out

But trouble began to loom over the expansiveness of the times and over these Olympian visionaries who must have sensed the first signs of Depression ahead. They sold out as urgently as they had bought in and made a good deal of it. The new owners who signed a mortgage for $1,166,000 were Mary Duke Biddle, her brother, Angier Duke, and a friend, Malcom Meacham. These New Yorkers were now the owners of Jupiter Island and the Hobe Sound Company.

On the surface, everything — and everyone — in Florida was looking up. The stars were smiling or maybe laughing. Then, two devastating hurricanes struck, only a year apart. The one in 1926 wrecked Palm Beach; the one in 1928 caused the Okeechobee disaster, drowning some 2,000 people. The storms marked the beginning of the bust in Florida, and by 1930 real estate was for the birds, and the birds were mostly buzzards. The Hobe Sound Company was on the rocks.

In New York, Mrs. Biddle's lawyers waited for the tide to turn. It never did. It just kept going out and out. Finally, in 1933, the lawyers advised Mrs. Biddle to sell. Her tax position that year was such that a financial loss — the larger the better — would make her better off! The lawyers wanted to show a big loss. They set the value of Mrs. Biddle's Florida holdings at $25,000. A group of young men in Mrs. Biddle's office jumped at the price. They bought

Building a green beside the sea. Third from left is George Blagg, the Island's first golf professional, succeeded by Gil Cavanaugh, 1959.

William S. Barstow (right) with Lucius Robinson and the Gordon brothers, Fred (left) and Bob. Note the broad expanse of beach.

her assets and sent one of their number — Forrest Hyde — to Jupiter Island to see what they had.

"See Mr. Barstow"

John Simpson was manager of the Inn. He showed Forrest Hyde what he and his friends had bought. It added up to a run-down resort that would require thousands of dollars in repairs and improvements, plus $40,000 in back taxes. Now it was Forrest Hyde who wanted out. John Simpson gave him a suggestion: *see Mr. Barstow!* That suggestion marked the beginning of the Jupiter Island, the winter colony, as it is today.

William S. Barstow was a retired utilities executive, a partner of Thomas Edison, who lived "down the Island" south of the Inn. Restless in his retirement, he wanted something to do and for some time he had had his eye on the Island Inn. When Forrest Hyde offered to sell (at no profit) the holdings his group had bought from Mrs. Biddle, Mr. Barstow shook hands at once. He was so pleased with the deal that he gave the Hyde group twenty percent of the common stock in the new Hobe Sound Company that he intended to organize.

William Barstow was a man of action. The next day he

Above: The Island's first golf course. Nine holes, sand greens, lots of mosquitoes and very few birdies. Later on, Dick Webel and Nat Reed came to the rescue with new landscaping designs.

Below: Harbour Island, 1920. No landscaping. No Japanese Bridge. Never underestimate the power of the ladies of the Garden Club!

called on three friends who lived on Jupiter Island. These were Arthur S. Dwight, Joseph V. Reed and Joseph Reed's brother-in-law, Samuel F. Pryor, Jr. Together, in 1933, these four formed the new Hobe Sound Company and began to put things in order.

Two years before, the Joseph Reeds had come on a month's holiday to the Olympia Beach Hotel with their 2-year-old daughter. Here, in Permelia's words, is a glimpse of the Island then.

"Picture a great jungle. The casuarina trees did line the roads but were a fourth of their present size. The only barren area was the 9-hole golf course. It had been built in 1920, 11 years before our arrival, and only a few palmettos dotted the course. The grass was not exactly grass, a mass of weeds, but the actual layout of the present first nine holes was the same then as today. No Christ Memorial Church, no Golf House, no dormitories, no River Road, no Beach House or Pieces of Eight. Only jungle, with the Van Voorhees house on one side of the first fairway, the Bassett houses backing up to the fifth and sixth fairways. On the beach side to the fork in the road, the former Harriman house (now the Ordway house), Cardinal Mundelien's (now the Kean house), the Dwyer house (now Mariner Cottage), the Stone house (now the Richmond house) jungle

in the middle, jungle to the north and to the south and on the river to the fork in the road. The Main Club and five cottages connected with it were there. The cottages were alphabetically named and built at the same time as the nine hole course in 1920. They were jerry built, poorly furnished and they had been left to run down.

"From the fork in the road south on the beach side there were two houses — the Mulford house and the Barstow Beach house, now the Offutts'. The river side had more homes beginning at the fork going south. But the owners were few — to be exact, seven in all. Mr. Barstow had bought three of the older houses. The last one on the river south was the Hildebrandt house, since torn down. A year after the founding of the new Hobe Sound Company Joseph purchased the shares of the owners and he really went to work."*

A little later we will tell how Joseph Reed went to work. But first, let's go fishing.

*In 1952 Joseph Reed decided to share the ownership of stock in The Hobe Sound Company with Island residents. The Reed family now own 60 percent of the stock. There are more than 160 other stockholders who together own 40 percent. There are ten Directors of the Company. Six of them represent the Reed family's interest. Four represent the "minority" stockholders. There is a provision that no assets of the company may be sold without the approval of eight of the ten Directors.

The Fishermen

The first houses on the Island were called fishing camps but actually were substantial homes. Joseph Jefferson, the actor, famous for his protrayal of Rip Van Winkle, had a fishing camp here in the 1890s. His friend, Grover Cleveland, who vacationed at Sewall's Point in Stuart when he was President, often came and fished with him. Charles G. Dawes, later to become Vice President under Calvin Coolidge, was an avid fisherman and had a house on Coconut Point. (Rumor has it that some of the earlier camps were more than fishing camps and were, in fact, hideaways for refugees from the formal life in Palm Beach. There were boats with names like *Monkey Business*, of recent memory, and patrons to match. All this, of course, was long, long ago.)

In 1894, Henry Morrison Flagler pushed his Florida East Coast Railroad to West Palm Beach, and in the same year he opened the Royal Poinciana Hotel, at the time the largest in the world. The next year he built the celebrated hotel, The Breakers, on the ocean. From those years forward Palm Beach was the place to be "in the season." Few wealthy people were able to resist its glittering appeal. But there were some who could, and several of them were hooked by the lure of fishing at Hobe Sound.

In 1925, a Virginian, Mr. J.D. Bassett, bought a house in Palm Beach. He was an avid fisherman and discovered the happy fishing grounds of Jupiter Island. He made the trip to and from Palm Beach so often that the captain of his boat said, "Mr. Bassett, you come up here almost every day. Why don't you just move up here?"

Mr. Bassett replied, "I think that's a very good idea." And so he did. About a year later another visitor destined for Palm Beach never even got there. This was Fred Gordon of Rochester, N.Y. He chartered an old houseboat, a paddlewheeler, in Jacksonville and started down the river. When they were passing Jupiter Island, Mr. Gordon saw a "For Sale" sign on the end of a dock. He looked the property over, and liked it so much that he bought it on the spot.

Tom Stanley, a grandson of J.D. Bassett who has a home on Jupiter Island now, remembers his aging grandfather's passion for fishing.

"Grandpa had a chauffeur and handyman. His name was Pete and he knew all there was to know about fishing in the surf. Each morning he would rise early, drive along the ocean from one end of the Island to the other. He would decide where the best fishing spots were for different kinds of fish — pompano, bluefish, snappers. Then he would get the proper bait, sandfleas or cut mullet, and get the fishing gear ready. At about nine o'clock he would drive up to the house and say, 'Let's go fishin'.'

"Mr. Bassett would then come out with his newspaper and get in the car and they would drive to that day's choice spot. If it was a hot day, they would park under the trees. Mr. Bassett would read his newspaper while Pete got things organized. He would take the long Calcutta rods and the bait to the beach, and then come back for the chair. This was a handsome mahogany chair that had no legs, just right for the beach. After Pete had placed the chair he would say, 'Mr. Bassett, we is ready go fishin'.'

"Here is the way Mr. Bassett went 'fishin'. He would sit in the chair and encourage Pete as he made the casts. When there was a strike and a fish was hooked, Mr. Bassett would applaud and say, *'We got it, Pete, we got it!'* When they got home, Mr. Bassett would point proudly and say, 'Look at the fish I caught.' (It was presumed that by this time Pete was putting the car away and so was able to keep his smiles and his thoughts to himself.)

Above: 1927, John D. and Pocahontas Bassett and a nice catch of fish. Their home is now the Don Grant house on Gomez Road. Left: Bassett brothers — J.D. and C.D. — with some big ones caught in 1925. Below: Tom Stanley's father, Gov. Stanley of Virginia, left, at the Bassett Creek Landing, 1935. Legend has it that "The fishin' was good 'til them Bassetts caught all the fish!"

"Mrs. Bassett also loved to fish. She would troll in the waterway for bass and snook, and in one way or another, there was always fish on the Bassett table — for breakfast, lunch and dinner.

"But fishing for bluefish was the big excitement. Nothing was ever allowed to interfere. On a super-bluefish day Pete would drive Mr. Bassett up and down Gomez Road, honking his horn. Mr. Bassett would lean out of the window and yell, 'The blues are running!' Then all less important activity stopped. Everyone would head for the beach. Even school stopped. No Latin, no math, no history — as long as the blues were running."

The Builders

Fishing was but one of Mr. Bassett's passions. Having his large family around him was another. J.D. Bassett was the founder of the Bassett Furniture Company in Virginia. He had four children. When he moved to Jupiter Island, he bought a large piece of land and built a house, the one that is now owned by Donald Grant. North of his house, he gave a piece of land to each of his children, and each of them built a house, so that now there are five houses in a row, each one occupied by a Bassett or a Bassett relative. J.D. had twelve grandchildren. All of them grew up on Jupiter Island. They all loved to fish, and many of them still do.

Another visitor with a passion for building was the Reverend Dr. George St. John. Dr. St. John's passion was of two kinds. He was Headmaster of the Choate School in Connecticut, which he had founded and which he owned. He loved to build character in the boys who were in his charge. And it turned out that he loved to build houses on Jupiter Island, a place he discovered on a vacation trip to Florida in 1933. It is certain that Dr. St. John avoided Palm Beach. His feelings about that resort were probably similar to those of the Reverend Endicot Peabody, Headmaster of the Groton School. At the beginning of each spring vacation, he would bid farewell to his students and say, "I hope you boys will all have a very good time on your vacation. *But do not go to Palm Beach, that den of iniquity!*"

On his 1933 vacation Dr. St. John went no nearer Palm Beach than Pompano. From there he drove North. He loved the ocean and whenever possible he drove along the keys on Route A1A. One day, he and his family found themselves exploring the beaches of an unknown island. They admired the view of the ocean and of the river. There was a fine stand of casuarina trees and, most startling of all, there was a sign beside the road: FOR SALE. Before many hours passed, Dr. St. John had bought a strip of land — 150 feet wide from ocean to river — for $4,500. This was his first, but far from last, investment in Jupiter Island.

Everyone warned St. John not to build a house on the ocean. But the Doctor knew what he wanted. He built a small house with a large ocean view, named it *Pirate's Pass,* and moved in. Then he looked around for more land. Other people came to Jupiter Island to fish or play golf. Dr. St. John came to build and to plant, to improve the land. He called it "pulling up a briar and planting a rose." He brought down some of the maintenance crew from Choate, and with their help he pulled up eight briar patches and planted eight houses, every one of them on the ocean. Some he sold, some he rented and sold later. The houses were attractive, and so were his names for them: *Pirate's Pass, Southern Seas, Thalelta (The Sea), Flotsam, Jetsam, Sea Urchin, Casa Canute.*

Dr. St. John built well. Edsel Ford bought one house, his brother-in-law Ernest Kanzler, bought another. George Jackson Mead, President of Pratt and Whitney, bought another, and so on. *Jetsam* remains in his family. It is owned and loved by his son the Reverend Seymour St. John, who succeeded his father as Headmaster of the Choate School and now is Associate Rector of Christ Memorial Chapel.

Above: Dr. and Mrs. George St. John. Headmaster of the Choate School. Below: Joseph Reed fishing, 1934.

Chief among the builders was, of course, Joseph Verner Reed. Perhaps the first thing to say about Joseph Reed is that, although he accomplished a great deal, he appeared to work without effort. Harmony and a cheerful atmosphere seemed to follow him wherever he went. In painting terms, he was an impressionist; it was light and atmosphere that counted. For quite a number of years, Richard Webel, the noted landscape architect, worked with Joseph Reed closely in the landscaping and redesigning of the entire Club area. He says this: "Through it all, Joseph Reed was a spring to keep things going. He had great imagination, and he knew the value of things — not just the cost of them. Everybody was always afraid that Joseph might spend too much. But his was not only a business transaction; his was making beauty and having great value as well. He had extremely good taste. His instincts were invariably correct. He was very bright, and he wanted the best. That's why we have what we have."

In the theatre Joseph Reed's great love was for Shakespeare, and this led him to found the Shakespeare Festival at Stratford, Connecticut. He was a theatrical producer, and he put his money where his heart was. Nathaniel Reed had a front row seat at his father's early performances on the Island and in later years he collaborated in them. He describes what it was like.

"My Dad never worried about the details of running anything. He saw the broad picture, so he wasn't troubled by any of the problems of day-to-day management or the necessity of reading a statement. He never read a statement in his life.

"You'd say, 'Well, the Company lost $156,000 last year,' and he'd say, 'Isn't that too bad? I'll just have to buy another piece of land.' And so he'd buy just enough land from the company to cover the amount the Company had lost that year.

"He saw very early — and very clearly — that it would be important to protect both the North end of the Island and the South end. I remember that I wanted to build a second golf course at the North end but Dad had reservations about it.

"He said, 'I want to keep the North end as quiet as possible. I like the size of the Island as it is.'

"At dinner one night he discussed it with my brother, Sam. He said, 'I would really like to make a gift.'

"This was to be a gift of 500 acres at the North end. I was put in charge of how to get it done. First we got the University of Miami to come up and do a botanical and biological survey of the lands north of Bridge Road. They really killed everybody's enthusiasm. There were too many bobcats, and they didn't like the miles of mangrove jungle and the various ecotones that are in that land. So we turned to the Nature Conservancy. By that time the Hobe Sound National Wildlife Refuge on the West shore

had been created, and so we added this land as a unit of the Hobe Sound National Wildlife Refuge.

"I went up there a little while ago. I took friends in the boat up the river, and there's nothing like it. There will be nothing like it — ever. It's a wilderness marvel, but it'll be really a marvel in fifty years — a hundred years from now. There's so little of that natural world left. Never did Dad make a better decision than that one. We saw thousands of birds on that little trip — all kinds.

"At the South end we were very lucky. Dad wanted to restrict building on Jupiter Island to single family homes. The owners of land at Seven Oaks and Isle Ridge loved Jupiter Island and they loved Dad, so it was easy to get everyone to agree to be single-family homesites. Otherwise, it could be all high-rise, like the Jupiter Inlet Colony.

"Further south, at what is now Blowing Rocks Preserve, was something else. It was nose-to-nose confrontation. Dad wanted to buy that land and keep it forever wild. But it was owned by some characters in Miami. High-rise developers. Big, big wheeler-dealers. Very tough. They sued to change the zoning. We won before Judge Sample but they appealed his decision.

"I had been in Tallahassee and I knew the best land-use lawyers. We hired Bob Ervin and they prepared to defend our position before the Appeals Court in Lakeland.

"We flew to Lakeland the evening before the hearing and stayed in a small hotel across from the courthouse, and it was the luckiest thing we ever did, the break that won the case.

"I was walking down the hall to my room and as I passed an open door a man called out, 'Nat Reed, stick your head in here.'

"It was the principal owner of the property, a former State Senator. He was lying across the bed with a full fifth of bourbon on his chest.

"I said, 'Senator, how are you?'

"He said, 'I'm gonna beat you in court tomorrow.' I said, 'I don't think you will.'

"He said, 'I'll make you an interesting proposition.' I told him I wanted to check into my room first, and I did and I asked the lawyers who were with me if I should listen to the proposition. They told me to take a yellow pad and go back. So I did.

"They were all in there, the big wheeler-dealer and his principals.

"They said, 'We'll make you the following deal. If you win tomorrow, we'll sell you the property for $200 a foot ocean to river. If we win, we'll sell you the property for $500 a foot.' I said, 'Well, that certainly is an interesting spread. How do you know we won't take it to futher appeal and go on to the Supreme Court?'

"They said, 'Look, we ought to end this. We're paying taxes on that piece of land. We don't see how we're gonna make any money down there on single family homes. We'll settle right now. We think $200 a foot is a fair deal for a mile of property.'

"Then I called Dad from the hotel room. 'What do you think I ought to do?' he said, 'Go in there and shake his hand; furthermore, produce a deed and make him sign it.'

"I said, 'How are we going to raise a million bucks?' He said, 'Don't worry about that. Go in there and get it.' So I went back and said, 'It's a deal. We shook hands on it and got a piece of paper out and signed it in front of the lawyers, got it witnessed. Weeks later the court ruled in our favor. I

Joseph Verner Reed, theatrical producer and Shakespearean scholar, is in New York. He telephones his home in Greenwich. Answering the call, Permelia Reed is surrounded by her family, left to right, Samuel, Adrian, Laurel, Joseph Jr., Nathaniel. Joseph was co-founder and President of the American Shakespeare Festival, also served in the Paris Embassy as cultural affairs consultant.

The old North drawbridge is no more. Built in 1911 as a swing bridge, this familiar landmark was replaced by a "modern" bridge in 1987.

called Dad and said, 'What are we going to do now?'

"He said, 'Your mother will raise the money.' And he and Mother had a meeting at their house that afternoon. The heavy hitters of the Island all came. They were all party to it and they sent out a letter to tell what they'd done. The good people of Jupiter Island raised the money in twenty-three, twenty-four days. Ted Oughterson, Bob Severson, the Club Manager and I took the check down to these characters in Miami, and that's how we got the land and we turned it over to the Nature Conservancy to handle it as a nature preserve. What a lucky thing that motel door was open! And how typical of Dad to say, 'Don't worry about it, go in there and get it.' "

The Little Red Golf Cart

You may expect to see it anywhere, any time. A smart little red carriage emblazoned with its distinctive license plate *PPR*. Its distinctive driver sits upright, head high, gracious, alert, observant. My dear, *how* observant!

If Joseph Reed was an impressionist, indifferent to detail, Permelia Reed is a perfectionist. She knows that in the big picture small things matter. *For want of a nail, dear boy.* Her sharp eye misses nothing. Her concern is both piercing and ubiquitous.

A visit to the wild fowl pond on the golf course is almost a ritual. Mrs. Reed likes to feed her flock — the wood ducks, the mandarins, the teal, the red heads. But, today, the feed box is empty. *I must tell Nathaniel! I see the new swans have arrived. A species that is said not to be aggressive. I* **do** *hope it's true. The last pair was a* **disaster!**

As the little cart goes from point to point its occupant sees beauty all around her, beauty that she has done much to evoke. But she also sees **vines!** In places the vines are climbing over trees, strangling shrubs and plants. *I* **must** *send another notice to the Bulletin! It is* **too** *disgraceful!*

On a winter night, 1943, beachfront dwellers were awakened by an explosion. A German sub had torpedoed a U.S. tanker offshore. Some 20 seamen jumped through flaming water and swam to the beach between the present Kelley and Isaacs homes, some in tatters, others naked, many badly burned. Islanders took care of the men until the Red Cross arrived. At dawn the tanker was still burning.

The little cart is in attendance at every town meeting. *I do wish more people would turn out!* And at the Chapel, of course — not only for Sunday service but to supervise, inspect and encourage the installation of a new terrace, a new walk, a new ramp. *The dear people who helped to provide all this must know how grateful we are!*

The new boardwalk beside the golf house terrace rumbles pleasantly beneath the wheels of her golf cart and the lady approves. *A vast improvement! And there's that **dear** little heron beside Nathaniel's lily pond. It's **so** good to see him again this year!*

She passes two or three houses that seem crowded together. *Zoning. Zoning. We must **never** relax our Zoning!*

The croquet court, the tennis courts, the Main club, the dock, the theatre, the Town Hall, the Square — especially the Island Club office and the Library — all may expect a visit any day, any hour. Also the Beach Club, especially when the young people are here at holiday time. *Alita's program for them is so much enjoyed!*

There are, of course, limits to the places a golf cart can go — to Banner Lake, for example, or Zeus Park, or Reed Park or even to Blowing Rocks or the North End. But there are no limits to Permelia Reed's devotion and she travels her domain by car. She is a doctor doing the rounds, a gardener inspecting her grounds.

The day begins early. Six o'clock. After a glass of apple juice, a cup of tea, a muffin and *The Stuart News* comes *The New York Times. How **could** one exist without it? (Arthur was such a **dear** man!) (I see that **dreadful** Mr. Mease is still permitting himself to smile!)*

Breakfast, the Times, a morning swim, and the telephone: *Dear Boy, how very clever of you! You **must** know we are so indebted to you!*

Dear Girl, what a charming idea! I'll speak to the Mayor (or the Commissioners, or Nathaniel or Rood or Gibbs or Gil or Jim or any one of twenty others) *at once!*

The telephone also serves to arrange meetings about the Library, the Bazaar (*My dear, our needlepoint is **priceless**!*),

the *Bulletin*, the beach and its problems, as well as to arrange little visits, little luncheons and dinners and social niceties of all sorts. It serves also at times to send sharp reprimands, suggestions that are more than suggestions. *(Never again, dear boy!)*

"The idea," Permelia Reed said the other day, "was that this would be a place where good friends could get together and relax and enjoy the tranquil atmosphere and all the pleasures Jupiter Island provides. We *never* contemplated a resort," she adds sternly, "and we do *not* consider it a *resort* now!"

In the earliest days Permelia was busy raising five children. Tennis, golf, sailing, fishing, bridge, little dinners, larger dances, picnics, plus children, plus Joseph and his ideas, this was Permelia's world until Pearl Harbor — December 7, 1941.

The pleasant life for the ladies of Jupiter Island slowed to a halt. The men, including Joseph, who joined the Army left for the Service. Permelia Reed took charge of things here. She managed the "Inn," a larger task than expected because people who normally would have traveled to Europe turned to Florida instead. She took Joseph's place on the Board of the Hobe Sound Company, and kept things running so capably that when the war ended she and her husband worked as a team until his death in 1973. Since then she has carried on in her accustomed, spirited style. As she tends her Island concerns and helps it to flourish, she knows that she is supported by the love of her children and her friends.

Four years ago, on the occasion of the 50th year of the family's stewardship of the Island, *The Bulletin* printed this tribute from one of Permelia Reed's admirers.

White sand, sea grape and bougainvillea vine,
Blue sky, hibiscus and Australian pine,
Warm sun, tall palms and ficus trees,
The scent of jasmine on the breeze.

A paradise is here, a place apart,
Nature become a work of art.
This jewel set between sea and waterway
Has shown for fifty golden years this day.

Here is a world as it should be,
Happy Islanders are we.
Others, hibiscus have and bougainvillea.
We, alone, have our Permelia.

The sentiment seems more than ever appropriate today.

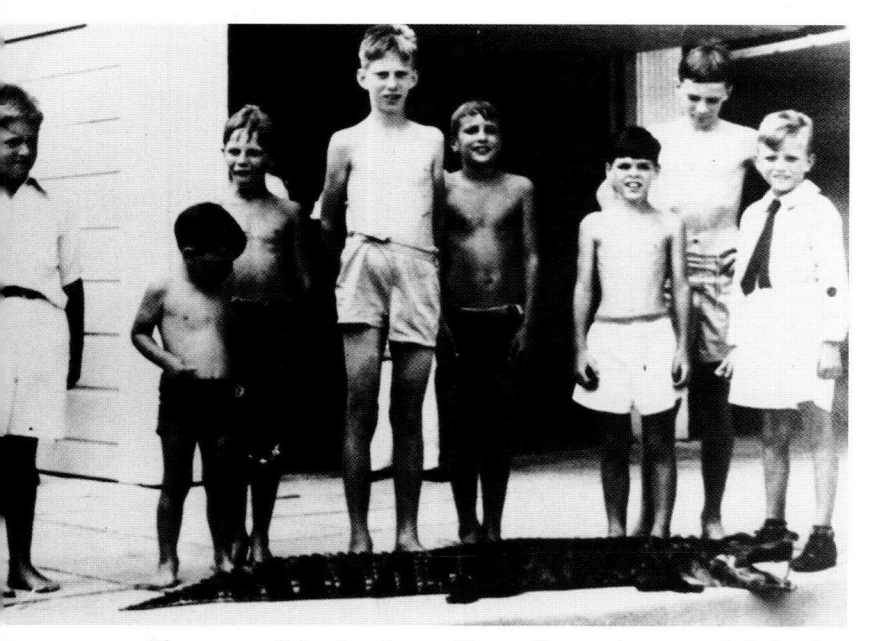

They were all having fun until an alligator interrupted their play. The intruder made the mistake of chasing Adrian Reed and was dispatched by Jim Black. The playmates are, left to right: Unknown, Tim Grant, Unknown, Nat Reed, Ted Hamm, Michael Grant, Adrian Reed, Terry Blanchard.

When We Were Very Young

Adventure at Bradley's

Fred Gordon remembers: "I was seven years old when my grandfather bought the house down here. There weren't many people on the Island. There were the Yates, of course. They were from Rochester and had the oldest house on the Island. And old Col. Murphy. He had that big house with the white pillars. And there were Mr. and Mrs. Barstow, of course. They were marvelous people. He had a white mustache and he always wore a celluloid collar. Never a soft shirt. Always a necktie, and I never saw him without a coat.

"Over on the mainland there was only the Post Office and

the water works. There was a little store called Godfrey's over at Olympia, but all he had was canned goods. We had to send to Palm Beach for groceries. It was quite a production.

"The caretaker used to get the order of the day from the cook. Then he would run over in a boat and meet the train to Palm Beach. He gave the list to the baggage man, and the next day he'd go over and pick up the groceries, plus the ice. If it was hot and the train was late, there wouldn't be much ice.

"The only fresh water we had was rain water. We had a great big tank — as big as this room — and that is what we took our baths in. We used bottled water to drink until grandfather put in a well on the mainland and piped fresh water over. That was about 1920. We had to make our own electricity, of course. We had a great big generator house. The room was from here to there full of storage batteries, but we had direct current.

"We had to make our own entertainment, too. My brother Bob and I were the only kids around. One day I decided to go for a sail. I had a flat bottom row boat and the wind was out of the northwest so I got a great big parasol. I got down the waterway as far as where Blowing Rocks is now, but I was too young to know that you can't get home against the wind with a parasol. I was pretty lucky, I guess. There was a marker out there so I tied up and sat tight.

"When it got dark and there was no Fred, the family went into a panic. They had an old Elko launch and they got the caretaker, they got the chauffeur, they got Father and started hunting. There were no searchlights on boats, but they had one of those things with mantles on it that they used to pull up. At about nine o'clock at night they found me tied to that marker.

"That was one piece of luck, and here's another one, some years later. I was down here for Easter Vacation in the thirties when the bank holiday came. They closed all the banks, and they wouldn't accept a check. They wouldn't accept anything but cash, if you had cash. Father and all the other men down here were trying to get home, and they had no cash.

"By luck, I had $100 in my pocket that was part of my allowance to come down here and buy my ticket. Young Fred Pryor, Permelia's brother, was a good friend of mine and we used to go to Palm Beach together to try our luck gambling at Bradley's. We decided that this was a good time to get some cash, so down we went.

"We started with roulette. We put $100 each on number 17 and it came up and we came home with five or six hundred dollars apiece! We were the most popular guys on the Island. I gave my father whatever it was he needed to buy his ticket home on the train. It was great to be young and foolish — and lucky — all at the same time."

The Little Red Schoolhouse

As the winter colony began to grow, so did the children. What to do about their education? They were too young to be sent to school in the North and too old to continue to be taught at home. (This was in the days when chauffeurs, butlers, valets, nannies, cooks, nurses and governesses were a normal part of Jupiter Island households.) In 1938 a few families, among them the Joseph Reeds, the Gene Tunneys, the George Mercks, founded a school on the Island. Some of the older kids had been enrolled in schools in the North, and those schools agreed to give them credit

The Schoolhouse, 1938. Classes were held every day, and discipline was strict — "unless the bluefish were running."

for attendance when they returned in the spring. In fact, the kids would come back to find that they were well ahead of their northern classmates!

The schoolhouse is now the home of Mr. and Mrs. William T. Finley on Links Road. It was little and red, and when the bluefish weren't running there was very good attendance. The reason for the excellence of the school was in the choice of the teacher. Miss Marion Stevens was a lady whom Joseph Reed had discovered and persuaded to take on the task of educating 10 or 12 youngsters who would rather have been swimming or fishing. The atmosphere was rather formal.

Ted Hamm remembers: "Each morning before school started the whole school would go out to the flag pole. You would place your hand over your heart and say the pledge of allegiance. And then the big kids would raise the flag. Miss Stevens would always be at the door to greet her pupils. She shook each child's hand. The girls would curtsy, the boys would bow, and class would begin.

"Miss Stevens was just a wonderful woman. It was such a small school that she could give individual instruction. She would call one pupil at a time, and you would get up in front of the desk — just you and she — and she would ask you the multiplication tables, the grammar, the history dates. She really taught you. She made you feel bad if you didn't do well. It was one of the best educations I ever got in my life.

"Miss Stevens was a real disciplinarian. Jim Pressly, the tennis pro, remembers that she would call him and tell him that a certain child hadn't done his homework that day, and Pressly co-operated. No tennis until the child went back and did his homework!"

The following item from the *Island School Record*, dated February 1, 1946, reflects the spirit of the school, the times and, incidentally, the condition of the beach 42 years ago.

"The older children went on a trip to Mr. Blodgett's farm. He showed them eggplants, squash, peppers, and beans growing. They saw people picking and polishing eggplants. Each child picked out an eggplant to take home. Mr. Blodgett started an irrigation pump so that the children could see how the farm is irrigated. All had a good time and thanked Mr. Blodgett for inviting them.

"Louise Copeland, Mimi Byers, Billy duPont, and Billy and Teddy Hamm came to school this week. Everyone is glad to have them.

"Mr. Joseph Reed invited a few children to go up the Loxahatchee River on Saturday. The trapper has three wildcats, two big rattlesnakes, and many others.

"Island School has collected 30 dollars and 50 cents for the March of Dimes. It went above the goal the school had set.

"The ocean is eating away the beach. At high tide there is no beach at some places. Mr. St. John's house had to be moved away from the beach.

"The Lockheed 'Constellation' flew nonstop from New York to Lisbon, Portugal in 10 hours and six minutes.''

A Boyhood On The River

Nathaniel Reed remembers: "We lived our entire lives as little kids at Artemis, our first house, which was well down the Island, and our lives were very simple. Almost every afternoon after nap we went down to see Grandmother Pryor. It was a long walk from Artemis, but it is still to this day one of the most enchanting walks on Jupiter Island, with Joe Jefferson's famous garden and on down to what is now the Kessler house. And then, of course, there was the beach.

"We were five little kids and the nannies and we went up the long driveway to the beach. There was a small, thatch changing-hut at the beach and my earliest memories are of the hours we spent building sand castles, knocking each other's castles down, and all the tom foolery that goes along with that.

"When we were very little, the big thing was the beach, but from the age of five on, the great excitement was fishing. Our wonderful caretaker, Andy Ondich (Uncle Andy), moved in next door to us and that was one of the best things that ever happened. Everything in the world that I liked Andy liked and we would go fishing every afternoon at four o'clock. The river was absolutely filled with fish. Nobody can believe how many fish there were. This body of water, the Indian River Lagoon, was at that time, without doubt, the most wonderful fishing spot in the whole Indian River. The Bassett-Vaughan kids adored to fish, all three brothers adored it, and it was just heaven. When we trolled we caught sea trout and when we bottom-fished it was snapper, sheepshead and grunts. All this was when we were living down at Artemis. They were wonderful, tranquil days, and it all ended very suddenly on December 7, 1941.

"I was eight years old, and the whole world turned topsy-turvy. Almost all the men on the Island, including my father, went into the Army, and my mother realized that if the Club was to survive she would have to get more involved.

"To be nearer the Club, we moved up to my Grandmother Reed's house, Liralay, and my mother took over control of the Inn. Only a few men were left on the Island, but there was one in whom my mother had complete trust. This was Grandmother Reed's former driver, Louis Wecker. He was a leathery, wonderful westerner who had worked for the Reed family from the time he had been a stable boy at the big house in Denver. Louis was getting on in years. He had a droll sense of humor and was a pretty stiff disciplinarian. He and I had fished together in Colorado on my annual visit to Grandmother Reed. He was the best fisherman, besides Andy Ondich, and he remains a bright memory.

"I had a marvelous bicycle rigged to a four-wheeled cart — a Red Ryder I think it was — and I had my two fishing rods and my net and my bait can. As soon as school was over, down to the dock I would go. I was old enough to have a boat now and I would get somebody to hold the net pole, and I would go out deep in the water and make a swing and pick up all these wonderful minnows and grass shrimp. We lived close to the dock, and I was out from morning to night, took a sandwich with me, never came in.

"The river was teeming: snappers and grunts, grouper and occasionally jewfish, spade fish, sailor's choice — the variety was incredible. Every other afternoon we trolled in the river with a little outboard motor, and the number of sea trout and channel bass was unbelievable. It was like being in paradise.

"One of the great jokes that Louis pulled on me was this. One day an immense manatee was rubbing himself on one of the pilings, causing the whole dock to shake and shiver. I didn't know what a manatee was — I thought it might be a fish. It was the largest fish that I had ever seen and I was determined to catch it so I went running into Louis' office and said, 'How do I catch that immense fish?'

"'Go get a bale of hay and rope and a hook,' he said, 'and we'll see what we can do.' I was halfway off the dock before I figured out that I'd been had. I came back and screamed at him, and that's when he told me it was a mammal, and a wonderful mammal at that. We went and sat next to the piling that the manatee was rubbing himself on and Louis gave me a vivid (if not entirely factual) account of manatees.

"And then there was Sherburn Prescott — a wonderful man, a wonderful character. I was introduced to Sherburn in 1941 at eight years of age. Neither my mother or father shot or fished, and they said, 'This is your Uncle Sherb.' From then on I shot and fished with Sherb all over the place. He was one of the original members of the High Point Club. I fished with him in Canada on the Restigouche for seven summers. He gave me my first two really fine pointing dogs. He left me his Duck's Print stamp collection, which I've kept up over these years.

"Sherburn loved anything to do with hunting or fishing. He had a tower at his house where he could look for pompano in the surf line. And he loved to collect rattlesnake rattles in ash trays all over the house. In those days we really did have a lot of rattlesnakes in the field, and Sherburn shot so much that he would have a vast collection at the end of the year. That — and breasts of quail. Don't ask me why he kept the breasts of quail, but they were posted on the wall when you came in, and then all of his famous poker hands were always matted and framed. He was extraordinary and a very, very dear friend. Andy Ondich, Lou Wecker, Sherb Prescott, I miss them all.

"Well, let me sum up. You can imagine a boy who loved butterflies, anything to do with botany, wild animals. A boy who lived on an island and to whom fishing was second to nothing in life. As I said, this was like growing up in paradise. I cannot think of a happier child in the world than I was living on Jupiter Island. I didn't care about anything else in the world.''

Palm Beach style on the Island. Left to right: Fred Gordon, Ward Wickwire, Jr., Bob Gordon. The "motor-man" is "Beacon." This photo was taken about 1920.

From Permelia's Files:

Bygone Scenes Stir Memories

Artemis was the Reed's home in the 1930s. Permelia and Joseph had room with the balcony.

Permelia with her first sailfish. Below, Laurel and Joseph; Permelia and Joseph building a sand castle.

Permelia with Joseph Jr. Next photo, Joseph Jr., Adrian and Laurel. The grandmothers, Mrs. Pryor (left) and Mrs. Reed.

Boating up the Loxahatchee; Joseph and Laurel on the beach; on foredeck with Alice Carson, Beezie Brownell. Masterwork in sand.

Joseph posed with his sons, (left to right) Joseph Jr., Nathaniel, Adrian and Samuel.

Joseph's 70th

The celebration was held in the main clubhouse. Guests from near and far came to toast their good and gracious friend and enjoy the party on this evening of January 22, 1972, Permelia's and Joseph's 41st year on the Island. The festivities were touched by Shakespeare and fond associations of time and place. The menu offered Tournedos Denbigh à la Sauce "Bard," Pommes Mignonnettes de Denver, Bombe Glacée Greenwichaise, Gâteau Joseph, Café Permelia and wines from Domaine de l'Ile Jupiter. *A Ballad for Joseph* interwove lines descriptive of Joseph with Shakespeare's verses from *Julius Ceasar*, *As You Like It*, *Hamlet*, *Anthony and Cleopatra* and others. The family put on a skit entitled "J.V.R. Superstar," and to still more applause, the elegant candlelit cake was brought in for Joseph to cut. Throughout dinner and after, there was dancing. Joseph and Permelia led the guests onto the floor in a very happy moment.

The Hobe Sound Story.

Boom, Bust, Steady Growth

by Norah Lind

It is six years away from the turn of the century. From the north Henry Flagler has just broken through the wilderness, laying a railroad which will pause in a place where no one lives, West Palm Beach, and continue on some day to the Keys. The great work train inches south; its dump cars are filled with rock and stone, its flatcars stacked high with ties and tracks: its big wooden sleeper and mess cars, with windows shut tight against the blazing heat, provide for the swarms of sweating workmen pick-axing and shovelling up the road bed. It is a clanging, noisy scene of progress, awakening the drowsing villages scattered along its path and connecting them to a new life. One of these, sitting luxuriously close to the Indian River, is Hobe Sound.

Every 20 miles or so along the new track, the Florida East Coast Railroad positioned groups of workmen known as sectionmen to maintain the tracks. These men settled with their families in existing communities whenever possible, and the six or seven deposited in Hobe Sound were a healthy boost to the population. They found none of the conveniences that Hobe Sound would someday offer its residents and Jupiter Islanders. Far off were the days of home deliveries from St. Onge's grocery, which at its peak had five delivery trucks and fifteen employees taking orders and delivering daily on the Island everything from kitchen staples to fresh caviar, leg of lamb and air-expressed capons.

There was a dirt crossroad when the sectionmen arrived, a few farmers and some Seminoles. The Seminoles lingered in Hobe Sound for several decades, and Sue Diamond, whose family founded and ran Diamond's Garage, saw a few of them in town as late as the '40s. She remembers the tourist attraction called Wild Bill's on U.S. 1. "Wild Bill had wild animals in cages and an Indian family who would wrestle with the alligator. The little boy went to school in Hobe Sound. He came in bare feet which fascinated my brother who wasn't allowed to go to school in bare feet. If you went to West Palm Beach to the dime store around Christmas time, you would see the Seminole Indians wearing their traditional clothing. They wound their hair around palms to build it up very high."

Wild Bill's wasn't the only source of excitement in those days; there was the notorious Ashley gang. John Ashley's family moved into the area in 1911, the same year that a Seminole, De Soto Tiger, was found murdered in the Everglades. John Ashley was accused of the murder which set off a string of robberies and plunderings by the Ashley gang throughout

In this old photo of Hobe Sound c. 1920 Godfrey's store, which also contained the post office, sits on an unpaved road that is

southeast Florida. They robbed banks including the one in Stuart and made money by any illegal method which presented itself, for years running liquor from Bimini and distributing it from a camp on Peck's Lake. Their center of activity shifted with their efforts to avoid the law, but they were often encamped at their house just to the west of town, near Fruita, a small clutter of structures which over the years crumbled to a scattering of old lumber. John Ashley, the undisputed leader of activities, had friends in the area, friendships nourished perhaps by the glamour of outlawry. But young Jesse Griffin, whose family was one of the first to settle in town, happened to be asked one night to stay to dinner at the Ashley house. Everybody sat down and said grace, and the story goes that the boy did not know who was sitting next to him until someone asked, "John, would you pass the butter?" Then, recognizing that he was seated next to the chief desperado himself, Jesse sprang from the table and did not stop running until he reached home.

Jim Black, long an employee of the Hobe Sound Company, took the outlaw in his stride, but he had a healthy respect for his abilities: "I rode with him on a mule-pulled wagon and he had his 45. A covey of quail came across the road in front of the mule and he (Ashley) stopped that wagon and shot six times and shot six quail right in the head — didn't hit them in the body, hit them right in the head. I know because I got out and picked them up."

John Ashley was killed in a shoot-out on Sebastian Bridge.

now A1A. The crossroad in the foreground leads on the left to the old water tower and on the right to the railroad tracks.

Next to him, also shot dead, was his cousin, Hanford Mobley and an unidentified member of the gang. The three were fitted into a common vault and buried next to three other Ashleys — two killed in the practice of their trade, one an infant — on the land where Mariner Sands now sits. Ashley's mother who wept during the service, lived next to the tiny cemetery. Later, when her home still stood there an abandoned reminder of notoriety, grave robbers periodically exhumed the bodies in search of loot.

Around the time of these midnight forays, the population of Hobe Sound boasted about 20 families. Thomas Fair, a former Island employee, came to farm in 1923: "To me it was just a real hell. Mosquitos! There were so many mosquitos that they would cast a shadow." And they were far worse inland, away from ocean breezes and during the summer when the seasonal residents of Jupiter Island escaped to the north. Fair fought them with smoke smudges. "We closed the door and windows and got a bucket and built a fire and let it smoke up the whole house inside. Then you could sleep." (The interior of every house in Hobe Sound was smudged with the same shade of gray. "We had one insect repellent that we used, but it was worse than the mosquitos. Coming down here on the railroad the train would stop in Ft. Pierce for 30 minutes and the guys boarding the train to sell Citronella would open all the windows. Mosquitos filled up the cars. The boys would come through yelling 'mosquito dope!' and they would sell out!"

Jim Black recalls the early days.

Fighting mosquitos was not the only thing that was going on. In fact, a boom, the famed Florida boom, was about to begin. It had been gathering in the more populated areas of the state, and now its fresh wind was stirring the air around the little mosquito-besieged town. Godfrey's store, the only two-story structure in town, supplied necessities. The post office was in the same building. A drug store, Diamond's filling station and a restaurant went up. And there was a great deal of buying and selling. Black recalls his cousin who "owned a piece of property from Bridge Road to the next street north where the library is now. He sold that piece of property seven times during the Florida boom. He'd take a $10,000 deposit and if you didn't show up in six days, you would default. He made $60,000 and still had the property. Well, it was all on paper."

The decision was made to pave the streets and sidewalks. Says Jim Black: "They bought three little tractors from Cleveland, Ohio, that were only about nine feet long. All they would do is dig themselves down in that sand and get stuck on the bottom. My old man said, 'If you get me about eight

Olympia sign atop Diamond's garage beckons customers to cafe next door (far right). The busy filling station offers Texaco.

41

teams of mules, sir, I'll grade those streets for you.' Dad graded every street in Hobe Sound that way, and every sidewalk."

Then the big-time came to town. A New York real estate firm bought the tract of land which included within it Hobe Sound and Jupiter Island. It was the Olympia Improvement Company, and one of its first moves was to change the names of Hobe Sound and Jupiter Island to Olympia and Olympia Beach respectively. It drew up a plan for the town that would transform it into a Grecian paradise with streets named Apollo, Juno, Mercury and Venus radiating from a park called Zeus. It sold lots, built several houses and began work on another fantasy called Picture City with the goal of moving Hollywood to Florida. As a starter it laid the sidewalks and erected the light standards.

When the Great Depression struck, everything collapsed, including even the new name. Gone were the Grecian and Hollywood dreams, and the light standards for Picture City are still standing forlornly along A1A. But over on the Island wrote Mahan in his book, *It Could Only Happen In a Small Post Office,* "The winter residents who owned the large estates, there being less than thirty then, went on giving their parties and...at one of these parties someone suggested that the name of the village be changed back to Hobe Sound. They drew up a petition; however, not being voters they had to circulate the petition among the merchants and voters on the mainland. The Olympia people wanted to keep the name Olympia, so they circulated another petition among the same merchants and voters. The merchants, not wanting to offend what few customers they had, signed both petitions." The two petitions were sent to the Post Office Department, which replied that it did not care what the residents called their town, but to please decide. They were also sent to the railroad which took the matter into its own hands and hung up the old Hobe Sound sign.

There were few jobs to be had; people left town to seek work elsewhere; the Olympia offices loomed blank and empty; as the months went on, food became scarce. "If a rabbit ran across the road," says Jim Black, "there'd be fifteen people after him because people were hungry. I've eaten 'coon and my mother could cook a 'possum out of this world with sweet potatoes. Everybody had chickens, and during the turtle season, four or five people went at night to kill one. Nathaniel Reed asked me one day, 'Jim, why did you eat those turtles?' I said, 'Because we were hungry!' Why else would you eat anything? And the manatees, we'd eat those too when we could get them. They're delicious. You could cook manatee meat that would taste like pork, ham, beef or anything you'd want. And the sea turtle's eggs made the best cakes you ever ate in your life. The bakeries would buy them off you. You could take 100 eggs up there and you were good for $30."

Recalls Eugene Ferguson, another former employee on the Island, "Bacon was three cents a pound, but we didn't have three cents to get it, so we hit the woods hunting gopher. The gopher would go into the hole and we would dig him out."

Families shared their catches of alligator, turtle or manatee,

Having debarked from the midday train in 1937, Islanders await Diamond's ''Bus'' (opposite page) to convey them to their front doors. A truck will follow the ''bus'' loaded with the big luggage. In 1967, after passenger service ceased, the station was moved west of town where it still stands — in its quaint gingerbread style — the office of an orange grove.

and one man's success fed the entire town. There weren't many to feed. "I don't think there were a hundred people left in the whole area," says Thomas Fair. "You could lie down on the highway and take a nap."

This dirt "highway" (Route 1) had been upgraded to a narrow strip of asphalt by 1930. But the auto trip north was still a long, arduous ride with delays at the one-lane drawbridges, flat tires, overheating motors, and the stack-ups of cars where passing was impossible. Most people, including Jupiter Island residents, preferred the railroad.

Riding the train was less of a struggle, though it jarred and rattled along, and the management of the railroad was determined to keep it running at all costs. Even after the 1928 hurricane left sections of tracks submerged, the trains pushed through the water with men walking in front of the engines testing with poles to see if the rails were in place. But no matter what the weather was, the trains ran late, which was always good stuff for the local humorists. In his book Postmaster Mahan tells about the train due in Fort Lauderdale at noon. The train was always late, but one day the bulletin board showed that it would arrive on time! It was unbelievable, and one of the town fathers decided that a celebration was in order. He called out the high school band and several local dignitaries for the ceremony. The train pulled into the station at twelve sharp, and the band struck up a tune. The engineer stuck his head out the cab window and inquired what was going on. He was informed that it was a celebration for his bringing a train in on time. The engineer laughed and said, "Hell, this is yesterday's train."

But as the years went by, the railroad improved greatly, and as more people used it coming south the Town of Hobe Sound snapped out of the Depression, grew and prospered. There were four tracks now instead of one, and at least four southbound trains passed through Hobe Sound every day. Up north men in coats, ties and hats and women dressed as if for a luncheon boarded trains bearing such names as the Champion or the Orange Blossom Special, and the ride from Pennsylvania Station in New York to Hobe Sound took about a day and a half. The designs of the locomotives had progressed in power and immensity, and now the giant six-wheelers were in command of the tracks, sounding the deep wail of their whistles at the road crossings south of Port Salerno, throt-

tling down, boilers panting, easing to a stop along the Hobe Sound station platform in a great hissing cloud of steam.

Back in the early thirties a blinking light was installed on U.S. Route #1 at Bridge Road, and a pastime of some of the kids around town was to count the number of times it blinked in a minute and calculate from that the number of times it would blink in a year. They delighted in recalculating each time the power went off to make sure the total remained unchanged. The blinker was a sort of monument, signifying the dividing line between despair and hope. It was there because of more traffic and more people and Hobe Sound was on the road to good times once again.

There was a weekly paper, *The Stuart News,* in which to read about the world outside. But Hobe Sound was, in a sense, a world in itself, one that included Jupiter Island just as the residents of Jupiter Island recognized the importance of their mainland neighbors. The two communities relied heavily on each other. Deputy Sheriff Arthur Broderick lived on the mainland and watched the Island closely in the off seasons: "Your house was checked a good many times every week. At the end of the month we sent a card to all the people telling them what condition their houses were in."

When Islanders returned in the fall and winter there were more of them each year who had discovered the beauty of the place. The Mainlanders with a head for business and a feel for the local market were busy. With $800 borrowed from Mr. Barstow, Jim Diamond, for example, started a taxi and car rental business headquartered in his garage. In 1937 he had a Ford cut in half and stretched by the Toledo Bus Works. Painted pale yellow with the familiar palm tree, the vehicle was nicknamed the "bus." So, with his stretch limo, the personable Jim Diamond brought a new Floridian style to his daily business of meeting the trains at the station. The Island families arriving for the season brought their pets, nannies, tutors, children, grandchildren, chauffeurs, maids, fishing rods, countless suitcases and trunks, and the Bassetts from Virginia, who had driven by auto to Jacksonville, brought the family car. The cats, dogs and people got into the stretch limo's five rows of passenger seats, rode off to the Island followed by Jim Diamond's truck piled high with the luggage. Jim made the trip so many times that he knew the characteristics of the Island staircases and how to manipulate the largest bags up through their twists and turns.

Diamond's taxi, car-rental and train-meeting service did ambulance work too. One high speed trip carrying a young black man who had been bitten by a snake, resulted in four blown out tires and a grand entrance to the hospital parking lot on the wheel rims. Nathaniel Reed had no sooner arrived from the north to recuperate from a boarding school bout with appendicitis, than he came down with the measles. Permelia struggled to tend to him and manage the Club. Just as Nathaniel was recovering, Samuel was stricken with appendicitis, then young Joseph the next day. Diamond rushed the two Reed boys to St. Mary's Hospital for appendectomies on two consecutive days.

A piece of engineering critical to the flourishing of the Hobe Sound-Jupiter Island scene was the bridge. The first bridge, built in 1911 when the water it spanned was still the meandering Indian River, was operated by hand cranks that swung the center section on a pivot. The next one, built after the river had been dredged and channelled to become the Intracoastal Waterway, lasted almost half a century. It was an electrically operated drawbridge with wooden planking that

Jim Diamond poses with the "Bus", his cut-in-half, stretched Ford, which was a well-known amenity around the Island. It met the incoming trains and in emergencies served as an ambulance.

Donald St. Onge and his sister, Joyce, pose by their father's first truck. It delivered staples and delicacies to Island homes.

rumbled under crossing cars and a mechanism of gears that groaned and clanked as the half-spans were raised and lowered while a warning bell clanged. Mr. and Mrs. Griffin operated the bridge and being friendly, agreeable people, the fishermen, passersby, kids off to the beach and whoever else liked to stand around for a while, exchange the time of day and help Grandpa Griffin mend his nets. One of the half-spans fell into the water in the late forties so the Griffins provided a boat. The Islanders loved this old picturesque bridge which broke down more and more as it aged; it was a most suitable entrance to the Island. Finally, in the mid-eighties, the higher, slightly looping concrete bridge replaced it.

Social life, of course, grew with the times and expanded from mingling on the bridge to, as Arthur Broderick remembers, "covered dish dinners on the beach. Then Mrs. Reed donated the Civic Center. Everybody would go to the Civic Center and play and sit and talk and shoot pool. On Thursday nights we would hire a little country orchestra and have a square dance."

World War II brought a lot of action to Hobe Sound. Camp Murphy, an Army Signal Corps operation, occupied the present site of Jonathan Dickinson Park. Up went a USO on Main Street, manned by local girls as hostesses and a committee of Town and Island women as chaperones. Diamond's busy taxi service made at least two trips a day to Camp Murphy bringing the soldiers to the USO. The war's end also brought a boost to Hobe Sound, because many soldiers stayed on, married, settled in the area. And Camp Murphy was useful in another way. Joseph Reed was stationed there, and when the place was dismantled he alertly trucked numerous barracks buildings and such to Hobe Sound for use as homes, garages, offices and to the Island as living quarters for the Club help.

Like Diamond's Garage, Clifford St. Onge's grocery became a Main Street landmark. It was a deceptively quaint store. Behind its well-stocked shelves and refrigeration units filled with every imaginable delicacy sat the 15 phone operators taking orders from customers mostly on the Island.

Donald St. Onge worked his way up in his father's business, starting as a delivery boy to Island homes, many of which ordered on a daily basis. "There were a lot of big parties.

Ten or fifteen fishermen sold us pompano and red snapper. In those days you couldn't give grouper away. We had caviar, wild rice; anything they wanted we had. Some people ordered the eye of the rib roast, just the eye...good business, nice trade, nice people."

After many profitable years, however, the cost of keeping a larger and larger perishable inventory began to eat into the profits. Don St. Onge explains: "We had a lot of refrigeration equipment. At that time you had to have a product on hand because you couldn't get it as fast as you can now. People would call up for large quantities. You had to have a large inventory and every year we put in new equipment. Our light bill was $350, then it got to $700, then it went to $1,200, then $1,800-$2,000 a month. That was a lot of money when you weren't doing anything in the summertime. Then chain stores came into existence. Business was hurt very badly and I could see the writing on the wall." Don, who now ran the business, closed the grocery and, moving along with the trends, opened a string of L'il Saints convenience stores. They did well for a decade or so until the large supermarkets came on the scene. Don St. Onge stayed at the cutting edge of progress and sold out. At present he is contented with a tailoring and clothes pressing establishment and a package-wrapping service for UPS customers.

The population of Hobe Sound continued to grow, and houses continued to spring up on the Island. The Islanders took a continuing interest in the mainland town and searched for ways to help it progress. In the '40s the Community Chest was organized to support numerous organizations in Hobe Sound. Today it provides much of the working capital for the Hobe Sound Child Care Center. It also contributes to the Banner Lake Club, the Hobe Sound Medical Center, local Boy Scout and Girl Scout Troops, the Hobe Sound First Aid Squad and the Volunteer Fire Department.

The relationship between the neighbors on either side of the Waterway has over many years been built on mutual respect and interdependence. There is warmth between them and quite a lot of caring. Islanders have given to Hobe Sound both in appreciation for what the town means to the Island and to keep its progress moving upward, which is good for everybody. Some of the gifts:

• The Community Presbyterian Church
• St. Christopher's Church
• Hobe Sound Historian Vee Chambers was given $1,000 every Christmas to play Santa Claus to the needy families in town.
• A playground for the black children. The black community had given the school board an acre of land on which to build a school before integration. The building was eventually torn down and the land was used as a playground. The county intended to sell the land since the black community had not included a clause in the original deed to insure that the land returned to their possession if it was not needed for a school. The community had paid $50 for the land, but the County now intended to start the bidding at $6,000. Roebuck Williams, a loyal Club employee, knew there might be someone who could help. "So one time I was parking cars and stopped Mr. and Mrs. Reed and told them the school board was going to sell our land, and we didn't have anywhere for our children to play. They would have to play in the streets, and I said that was bad. Mrs. Reed said, 'That is bad. Joseph, see what you can do about it.' The Hobe Sound Company had to give the school board two acres for us to get just one."

- The Banner Lake Club. It provides assistance to the area's residents who are black: clubhouse and lake, baseball, basketball, a Meals On Wheels program for the elderly.
- Reed Park with baseball diamond and tennis courts.
- Land for the public beach at Bridge Road.

At Joseph Verner Reed's death, Banner Lake Village, Inc. was established with the contributions of close friends. The memorial fund is administered by John Duberg to maintain the Banner Lake area. One year the fund paid to remove 75 dilapidated homes.

The Hobe Sound Company has made many gifts to the townspeople including the land on which the Hobe Sound Child Care Center was built in 1969. When the building was destroyed by fire in June, 1984, it was replaced a year later with a completely updated structure, funded largely by the Community Chest plus some insurance money and donations.

So, the mainland progressed through its own efforts and those of the Islanders who lent a hand. Joseph Verner Reed could sense the needs of the people before they knew themselves. When Roebuck describes Mr. Reed's kindness, tears come to his eyes. "If you walked by him and called his name, it made no difference who you were, he would stop and listen to you and consider what you had to say. If he wanted to give you something he had a way of saying it. He gave me something one time and he said, 'Roebuck, my boy, how would you like to take this out of my life and put it in yours?' "

How Hobe Sound Got its Name

The origin of the name Hobe Sound is not entirely clear, but the consensus is that it comes from the Spanish word Jobe (pronounced Hobay), the name the Spaniards gave to the supreme god in Roman mythology. During their exploration of Florida they named the body of water that is now called Jupiter Inlet after the mythological god, calling it Rio Jobe and the Indians in its vicinity, the Jobeses.

An English map, printed in 1671, clearly shows the name Hobay marking a place in the general vicinity of Hobe Sound. The belief is that Hobay — sometimes written as Hoe-bay — was the Englishman's rendering of Jobe and that during many years of English usage the Spanish inflection, "bay," was droped and the name anglicized to Hobe, pronounced as it is today. The Spanish-to-English transition from Jobe to Jupiter is natural enough and explains later local borrowings from mythology — Juno Beach, Olympia Improvement Co., Zeus Park, etc.

Joseph Verner Reed distributes garbage bags to young friends cleaning up Banner Lake section of Hobe Sound.

Great Weather

With Occasional Exceptions

by Cecil McIver

"The weather on Jupiter Island is FINE." That's official! Mrs. Reed declared it to be so in December, 1977.

Observations over 40 years had shown her that "It may range from clear and sunny to fair and warm: it may change from scattered clouds to blue skies. Look for weather that's warmer than Minnesota, clearer than California and fairer than your own." Her framed declaration may be seen hanging near the front desk of the Main Club building. And the weather is FINE, generally speaking. The mean temperature month by month is shown below:

J	F	M	A	M	J	J	A	S	O	N	D
64	60	70	71	75	82	83	83	81	78	72	66

The highest and lowest temperatures in any month rarely deviate from the mean by more than 10°, making it a very equable climate.

Just occasionally, Jupiter Island has had not-so-fine weather and has experienced tornados, freezing cold, storms and hurricanes. While tornados are common in Florida, they generally have been small in this area and have caused little damage. In 1980, for example, George DuManoir was sitting on his terrace reading the paper when he heard an unusual noise — "a kind of whoosh", he said — and he folded his paper, got up and went inside the house. Moments later a tornado rushed by, knocking over trees and breaking glass windows on the terrace. No one was injured. As quickly as it had come the tornado disappeared, leaving a swath of damage about 30 yards wide.

Freezing weather of any significance also has been infrequent. During January and February the temperature at night occasionally may dip below freezing for a few hours, but residents have been able to cope with this by protecting their more delicate plants or moving them indoors. The worst freeze on record occurred in 1895: Jupiter Island was part of a pineapple plantation then; the pineapple crop and the company which owned it were ruined. In 1984 another serious freeze occurred with temperatures of about 28° lasting for several hours on several nights. It caused widespread damage to trees and shrubs; many of them died. The usually lush vegetation looked as if a defoliant had been sprayed over it; green gave way to brown as the dominant color; trees raised their limbs to the sky in silent complaint, and houses which had remained hidden demurely behind their screen of vegetation suddenly became starkly and unhappily visible. On the mainland orange groves were destroyed and abandoned.

The appearance of the Island after the freeze provoked a strong reaction from residents. Right off they set about cleaning up the damage, relandscaping extensively and planting shrubs and trees that are cold-tolerant. In addition to this individual effort, a joint scheme led by Mrs. Reed came into being to clear and replant the northern and southern approaches to the Town. The Hobe Sound Company had donated the land for green space and the Islanders donated the money for new shrubs, trees and the landscaping work. Now, at this writing, the Island not only has regained its former appearance but in many areas its beauty has been enhanced.

Hurricanes (storms with wind velocities of 75 m.p.h. or more) are the major threat to the Island. They vary greatly in frequency (none in 1890, 21 in 1933) but during most years there are several storms, a handful of which will develop hurricane strength. Happily these usually have missed Jupiter Island completely or have brushed it lightly. All hurricanes are bad — winds of 100 m.p.h. or so are bound to cause damage — they usually are classified as "bad" only if they pack sustained winds of 150 m.p.h. or more. By that criteron, this region of Florida has had "bad hurricanes" in this century in 1910, 1926, 1928, 1938, 1949, and 1979. Some of these caused only a little damage on Jupiter Island but struck disastrously elsewhere. In 1928,

Trees in the garden of the Chatham house in Bassett Row (above) were blown down or snapped in two during the hurricane in 1938, and some fell onto the roof. Only the solid house construction prevented massive damage. The Island has never experienced a ''direct hit'' from a hurricane but only glancing blows from storms whose centers passed nearby. Long may our good luck last!

for example, floods accompanying the hurricane poured with immense force and speed into Lake Okeechobee, burst the retaining dike and drowned more than 2,000 people. That storm is described by Lawrence E. Will in ''A Cracker History of Okeechobee.''

''Sunday morning dawned here cloudy, but it was cool. The breeze before a hurricane is so gentle, sweet and cool that if you weren't half scared you'd feel plumb good. But this morning we didn't know enough to be ascared. Saturday's paper had said that the storm was headed for the lower East Coast...But you was axin' what's hit like to be in a hurricane? Well son, I'll tell you what hit was like in '28, you'd wish a thousand times that you was somewheres else. First off, you're a-settin' there in your house. Hit's black dark outside. The rain's a-dashin' agin the winders like a hundred fire hoses all to once. The wind's a-howlin' like a pack of devils turned a-loose, and that house is shakin' like a fisherman with malary. Then your roof goes sailin' off, and first news you know your house goes too, and there you are a-fightin' that black water. Now and again your foot hits bottom and you know you're travellin' fast but you don't know where, nor care much either, so long's you can just keep afloat. A tree limb ketches your shirt and pulls you under till your lungs is fit to bust. That's when you think your time had came, but you tear a-loose and keep on swimmin' for a right long while. After what seems an hour or two you hit on something solid and you climb up. Hit's a ditch bank, but you don't know where, you thought you was in the lake. So then you shiver in that sharp wind wishin' for a coat or a shirt or just anything. Then after the longest night you ever seen, hit sort of gets daylight but there ain't no sun, just low scraggly rain clouds trailin' their tail feathers across

that empty sawgrass marsh. You look around for a house, a tree, or maybe a telephone pole, but you can't see nothin' but mashed down sawgrass and low hangin' clouds, and now and again a shower of rain. So you take a chance and head off through the sawgrass and the water blamed near hip deep, and atter a right smart while you manage to git to town, what's left of hit. You go to the hotel, the onliest building in town which ain't ramshacked and tell 'em you're still alive, and would be mighty proud to have a bite to eat. And that's what hit were like in that storm of '28.''

The worst storm to hit Jupiter Island in living memory was in 1949, Friday, August 26th. The "Jupiter Island Mo" "published every once in a while by W. Mo., B. Mo. and Geron I. Mo. (subscription free)'', tells us about it.

"During this blow the wind recorder at Jupiter Light showed one hundred sixty-two miles per hour and then quit...Just in case you have never been through a hurricane we will quote from Chief Broderick's police report of that day: 'I reported for duty at five-forty a.m. Storm warnings had been hoisted from Vero Beach, south. I made one round on the Island and then began checking all homes to make sure everything was in order. Talked to some of the caretakers and they all seemed to have everything in readiness. About 8:30 a.m. we were warned the storm would come in between Fort Lauderdale and Vero Beach. About 3:30 in the afternoon a few trees began to fall. Some wires had fallen and one started a fire just south of the Brownell cottage. Allabaugh, special policeman, and I took care of this. I contacted Woods about 5:45 and told him it was no use to come out that night as I would patrol as long as I could and then get off the Island. It was beginning to get rough as I left the McConnell cottage where Woods

High wind and a building sea are threats to the Island's beach. A far greater danger to the entire Island is the hurricane with a tidal wave, which we have been spared so far, coming with it. Screaming wind in the hurricane of 1928 ripped off roofs in Hobe Sound (above), reduced some houses to matchwood and broke telegraph poles. Fallen power lines were a major hazard.

was staying but I checked the best I could on my way north. My last check was on the north end as far as the Bullock cottage. It was then 7:00 p.m. I took a look at the Quonset Hut of the Coast Guard and that was beginning to dance around. I prayed, and I am not ashamed to admit it, that I would get off the Island. I made it until I reached the other side of the tracks at which point the wind turned the police car with me in it completely around. Don't ask me how I made it home.'

'At 11:00 P.M., we were once more able to leave the house and Allabaugh and I patrolled the town for the remainder of the night as most of the business places had windows broken in. We tried to make it to the Island but that was impossible as we could only get halfway between the tracks and the bridge.

'At dawn Saturday morning workers were able to make their way to the Island. The south bridge was open when the power failed so we had no worries there. The north bridge was closed and Woods and two special police were posted there to stop sightseers and all others not working on the Island, as windows were out of many of the cottages and patrolling was impossible. I continued on duty until 12:20 p.m. Sunday, but couldn't take it any longer. Crowe cut his vacation and arrived back Sunday night. If this sounds jumbled please forgive.' "

To see the picture on the third day after the storm let us quote from a letter by Mr. Baird to Mr. Blanchard:

"On Sunday night I got a telegram from the police that my house was badly damaged. On arriving at West Palm Beach Monday I tried to get a cab to take me to Hobe Sound but they said they could not get through, so I took a Greyhound and they made it. From Route 1 someone gave me a lift to the Island. At the bridge I was very much pleased to be stopped by special police. I finally satisfied them I had a home there and was going to it. Soon Mr. Kanzler's truck came along and the driver said he could get down Gomez Road, so down we went and he let me off at your driveway. Well, Scotty, I had the hardest time getting through your yard over the Beach Road. Trees were piled across your drive as high as I am. On

Beach Road it looked as if one of your timber crews had been working for several days trying to cover the road with trees.

"It was a sorry looking place that Monday but when I left there a week later Beach Road was open, the work of clearing the golf course had been started and every one was taking hold in a wonderful spirit.

"Scotty, I want to tell you that I think the police did a magnificent job. Our house and a number of other houses were open to any one to walk in, but as far as I know there was no pilfering or loitering and all the men were most co-operative. Police were kept on the bridge until Saturday by which time most all cottages were closed in. I feel the residents of the Island have a great deal to be thankful for in the way this matter was handled."

Hurricane David, in 1979, was relatively mild, (90 m.p.h.) and it struck at low tide. It occurred in August (80% of hurricanes occur in August, September or October); there was ample warning; relatively few residents were on the Island, and it was possible to evacuate the Island in an orderly manner. (A few residents refused to leave the Island.) We boarded up our doors and windows, emptied refrigerators, packed emergency supplies of food, water, wine,

"The Great Thanksgiving Storm" in November, 1984, brought exceptionally high tides causing the Club dock to disappear and a golf cart to go amphibious on an adjacent road.

flashlights, clothing, books, etc. and headed inland. One group of residents, about 20 in number, rented one whole floor of a hotel in Palm Beach Gardens and established a commune there for the duration of the storm. We shared bedrooms, food, wine and reading material and had an amusing time. Since we had brought our most precious and delectable items of food with us we had a rather bizarre diet for a couple of days — the choice of caviar, smoked salmon, tinned grouse, etc., and exotic wines for breakfast, lunch and dinner! When we returned to the Island we found less damage than we had expected: many trees were down (Tom and Norah Lind lost 16), roads were blocked in several places, and power lines were down, but there was only minor damage to property. No one was injured.

It is to be hoped that our good luck will last, but we should not count on it. People who have not experienced a hurricane may not be able to comprehend the damage a bad storm may cause and there is the fear that good luck may have engendered apathy or a devil-may-care attitude which could be fatal in a future hurricane.

In violent storms loose objects may become lethal missiles, and even heavy objects can be moved great distances. In 1926, a resident of Hobe Sound was all but decapitated by a flying sheet of corrugated iron. In 1936 the roof of Mrs. Stead's shop at the Beach Club was blown off. There are records of a 1 x 3 pine board being whirled through the air with such force that it transfixed a mature palm tree like a spear, and of a 150 lb. lead weight being blown 600 yards! If Jupiter Island were to receive a direct hit from a bad hurricane, with winds in the range of 150 m.p.h. for several hours, we could expect tremendous damage from the force of the wind, from flooding due to torrential rain, unusually high tides and tidal waves up to 15 feet in height, and from falling trees, flying debris and broken power lines. Almost certainly, roads would be blocked and the bridge might become impassable.

In 1984, we had freak tides for a couple of days: a 20-knot wind had blown steadily from the northeast. The water in the Intracoastal Waterway at high tide rose at least 2½ feet above its customary level and 18 inches above the dock. Sea boots were useless because the water came over the tops. Those of us who lived on boats had to take off our shoes and socks, roll up our trouser legs and wade ashore! But occasions such as these and tornados and storms and hurricanes and freezes are so very much the exception that the weather on Jupiter Island is, indeed, FINE.

Album
in the
Sun

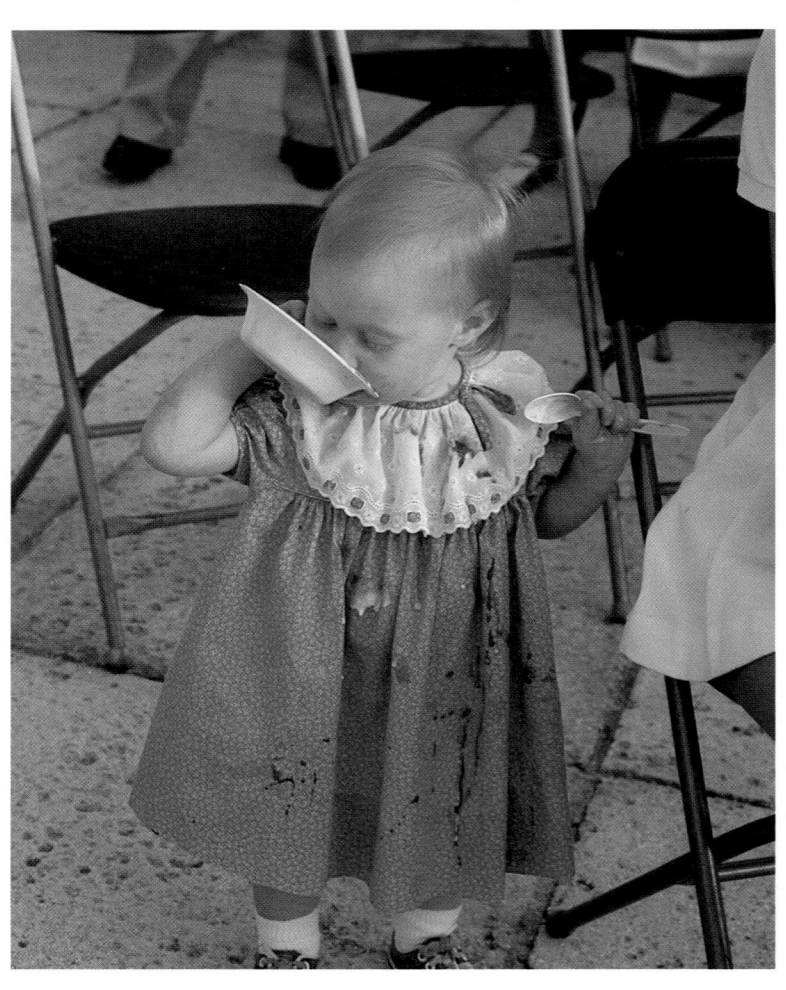

End of a Day

The Memorial Garden was given by Permelia Pryor Reed in memory of Joseph Verner Reed. Trumpet vine and bougainvillea adorn this Eden of remembrance, hope and thanksgiving.

House of Prayer for All People

by Seymour St. John

There was no church on Jupiter Island before 1939. During the season, four o'clock Evensong was held on the lawn of "Mother Pryor's" house overlooking the River, led by an imported curate singing to an imported organ, followed by tea and cookies. And so it was that Françoise Duclos (Mrs. William) Barstow determined to build an Island Chapel.

Almost from the beginning, Jupiter Island has been the beneficiary of strong-minded, competent and generous women. Given by Mrs. Barstow in memory of her sister, Laura Fontenay Delespine Duclos, Christ Memorial Chapel is no exception. I have often wondered if it were just by chance that the stained glass window over the altar depicts a scene which, except for one angel, includes only the haloed fair sex. It was Mrs. Barstow's thought that this would be the true Island church, its doors open to members of every denomination, residents and guests. As such it has played a special part in the life of the Island. Aside from regular services, almost 100 families have brought their children here to be baptized; another 100 have chosen to be married at the chapel altar; and others rest from their labors in the lovely Memorial Garden.

The original architecture — a warm Spanish style of stucco with a pink tile roof — has survived two face-lifts. By 1956 Mrs. Barstow, who loved to build, found plausible excuses to do so: 1) the new electronic chimes equipment cramped the sacristy; 2) an older congregation was uneasy with no lavatory facilities; 3) the seating capacity of 150 was too small for crowded Christmas and Easter services. Into the breach stepped architect Kemp Caler, who wisely chose a Spanish Mission style in extending the nave and adding a bell tower from which the amplifiers could peal for the Westminster chimes.

"The Chapel," says Caler, "was an extension of Mrs. Barstow's personality. She was deeply involved with every aspect of the construction."

"Was she easy to work with?"

"Very — as long as she had her way!"

Lovely interior of the Chapel and gifts of the people — the Anne Olin organ, the McConnell chimes, the 200 needlepoint kneelers — all symbolize the beauty of worship.

The Chapel was consecrated on March 13, 1939 by Bishop John D. Wing; and on March 19th my father, Dr. George St. John, preached the first sermon. His text was a favorite passage from Ecclesiasticus: "If thou seest a man of understanding, get thee betimes unto him, and let thy feet wear the steps of his door." But, "let the counsel of thine own heart stand; for there is none more faithful unto thee than it. For a man's mind is sometimes wont to bring him tidings, more than seven watchmen that sit above in an high tower." He and Mrs. Barstow saw eye to eye.

In its strategic setting, the Chapel looks out on a casuarina-lined fairway of the golf course, appropriately tying together Creation and recreation. It has even been suggested that at the morning offertory the plate be extended to the seventh tee. There are, however, hazards. Some still recall the morning following the recessional hymn and awaiting the benediction when, loud and clear through the open doorway, came the voice of a young lady who had just badly sliced her tee shot. The language was both memorable and theological.

Bishop Robert E. Gribbin of Western North Carolina set

As the sunlight sweeps over it from the west, the Chapel, a building of simple and inviting elegance, displays the additions of 1987 designed by Richard Webel. They are the Thanksgiving Terrace in the foreground and the ramp slanting up gently from the eastern side, lifting the entrance to the level of the nave. From the terrace, a brick, shrublined walkway extends east to Beach Road and west (below) to Gomez.

comprehension and fulfillment of its mission.

The spirit of the Chapel moved outward too from such vestry leaders as Lady Ramsey, Warner Baird and Rear Admiral Richard Tuggle, still acting in an honorary capacity after 35 years of service, ever present to welcome all comers to the Chapel steps. Another such leader, always in a quiet way, has been Mrs. Houghton Metcalf, for many years chairman of the music committee. Her approach bespeaks the heart of the Chapel, touching with loving concern the lives of musicians and choristers. Who could forget the days when during services her chauffeur babysat for the organist's four small children; or her weekly pre-church coffee klatch; or her Christmas parties with presents for all; or the use of her beach house for swimming and picnics; or her care for each member in sickness or trouble? And, inevitably, the music was correspondingly fervent.

That the spirit (I offer the choice of a capital or a small "s") affects a widening Island population is open to conjecture. And yet I permit myself the story of a couple from another attractive Florida haven who visited our Island last spring. They spoke of finding a noticeable difference here in community feeling and, in trying to account for it, concluded that it stemmed from the role of Christ Memorial Chapel. A happy thought.

the tone of the Chapel during its first twenty-five years. He was a "people" man, beloved by his flock, who believed in the good of all; and, as ultimate testimony to his faith in humanity, he remarried at the age of 91. Since his time the Island has been unusually fortunate in his successors. If I may skip from alpha to omega, our current chaplain John M. Allin, 23rd Presiding Bishop of the Episcopal Church, has not only captivated the congregation with his spiritual depth and outgoing humor, but has brought the Chapel to a new maturity both in organization and in the

Tennis, Everyone!

Editor's note: The players in action on these pages are the best of the Resident Club members playing here in the year 1988. Bill Nutting (left) and his wife, Pauline (far right) have accumulated several shelves full of Round Robin trophies while the Chairman of the Tennis Committee, Bridg Griswold, about to execute a net shot (lower right), has won quite a few himself. There are, of course, other good players on our courts today, but, alas, there isn't room on the pages for everyone. As for usable photographs of the fine players of the past in action — and there have been many on these courts — our research has turned up none. It has been suggested that not-so-good players — and duffers too — should grace these pages. Possibly. But speaking as one of these, I would suggest that most of us would be willing to forego that honor. As Jim Pressly says, "It's better to be lucky than good."

From the earliest days tennis has been an important fact of life on Jupiter Island. Nathaniel Reed remembers:

"The afternoons began at 2:00 when the Reed boys were all scheduled to play with the great pro that Joseph Verner Reed (JVR) had attracted to the Club. He was Arthur Rudolph, or Rudy, who was a super Hungarian. He lived with us during the war; a fine teacher, a beautiful player and a charming gentleman. Then, at 4:00, the courts were quickly cleaned, and JVR and his afternoon match came on. Rudy was in charge and would always see that JVR won, which was terribly funny.

"Then there is the story of Ted Oughterson. In 1935 Ted had begun to practice law in Stuart, and one day he got up enough gumption to drive down to Jupiter Island and up the long driveway to Artemis, which was quite an imposing building. He knocked on the door and Joe Lewis — our wonderful black butler — opened the door. Ted said: 'Would you let Mr. Reed know that Mr. Oughterson is here?'

"JVR was working at his desk and came out and met Ted and took him back into the living room and sat down. 'I'm a lawyer,' Ted said, 'and there's not much work. If there is anything I can do for you in Hobe Sound, please let me know.' JVR interviewed him for a while and then said, 'Mr. Oughterson, it was very nice to meet you and if we have any need for a lawyer, we will take you under consideration.' As Ted was walking out the door, he said, 'Mr. Reed, on top of being a lawyer, I play a pretty good game of tennis.' JVR said, 'I'll see you at 4:00 this afternoon.'

"Ted Oughterson became not only the Hobe Sound Company lawyer, but the Reed family lawyer and one of the closest friends the Reed family ever had. JVR and Ted played as much as five days a week per winter for years. Ted had an interesting post-tennis routine. He never showered down here. He wrapped himself up in towels, put on the same elegant polo coat and then came by — both at Artemis and later at Corsair — to have one glass of beer and reflect on the match. JVR had his cup of

Jim Pressly, head pro for 40 years, is the learned lodestar of Jupiter Island tennis. His impromptu scholarship on the subject of the game and the magnetism of his enthusiasm for it have drawn to the Island a galaxy of stars glowing with aspirations. He comes from a family of teachers in DuWest, S.C., where he went to Erskine College, thence to Columbia University and an MA in American History. He returned to Erskine ("My family were all teachers there.") and taught English and History. After a year of this, the tennis court lured him away from the lecture hall. Until World War II he taught tennis in Florida and the New York area and did some academic tutoring as well. He joined the Army as a Private, served in Europe for 30 months and rose to the rank of Captain. In 1947 Captain Pressly came here.

tea; Ted had his beer and then drove back to Stuart. It's hard to imagine two men who had a better time with each other and who liked each other more. They just loved their tennis.

"Tennis was very important because the golf course was nine holes then, and if you wanted eighteen you went to Seminole. There were some athletic guests — the Phil Turnbulls, the Don Grants and others — who were sort of heroes to us when we were kids. They would play a three set tennis match in the morning, have a swim, go to Seminole and play eighteen holes of golf in the afternoon, and then back for dancing at the Club. That was considered the absolutely perfect day.

"Rudy went back to Hungary in 1947. He was killed by the Communists, which was tragic. And that's when Jim Pressly, whom JVR had known during the war (Captain Jim Pressly — one of the best looking of all men) came into our lives, replacing Rudy as head pro, and has been here ever since."

Jim Pressly remembers:

"When Arthur Rudolph left, his son Arthur Prochaska took the job. After one year he was succeeded by Harold Duncan, the brother of the Duncan Sisters, a well-known acting duo in those days.

"He lasted two years, and then I got the job. I was out watching the Nationals at Forest Hills that fall before I came South when this wild looking character tapped me on the shoulder. It was Harold Duncan. He said, 'I hear you have the Jupiter Island job. You're not going to like it.' I asked him why not, thinking he would say there

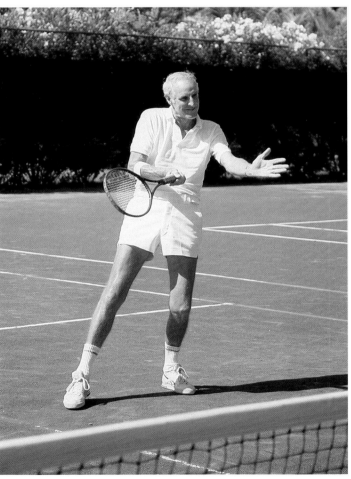

Herb Stead, a great Pressly find, is an exceptional teacher of players of all ages. He taught at the Club for 25 years, is now retired.

was no money in the job, or that I wouldn't like the people. He said seriously that the food was lousy. I laughed so hard that I was afraid they would hear me on the Stadium Court.

"When Mrs. Reed hired me, she said, 'The best player and the best teacher in the world could be a flop at this Club. We want somebody who can get good people to play and to encourage them.' And that's what we've always done. We try to see that people have good matches and good fun.

"When I came to the Club in 1948 there were five courts. Now there are fourteen. We added one more down by the tennis shop and eight more up on the higher land toward the Beach Club. The eight courts up there are sitting on a ridge of sand twenty feet high, and I think without a doubt they are the fastest drying clay courts in the world. We flood them every night to keep the surface firm. One evening the manager of the public courts in Stuart was here, and he saw that the courts were under water. He said, 'When are you going to use those?' 'Tomorrow morning at six o'clock.' He couldn't believe it. That is one reason why our tennis courts can be used so constantly.

"At first the season was exactly three and a half months. I reported for duty December 15th. We opened the shop December 15th and we closed just after April 1st...and that was it. Now it's practically double. Now we're open six and a half months.

"Tennis has become more popular every year. Not only here but everywhere. When I first arrived I was the only pro between Palm Beach and Daytona. In Vero, there was the Riomar Club — they had a couple of courts there. In Stuart there was nothing. I remember they had three courts in the middle of town, and a hotel out on the river with one or two courts. I had one assistant, Bob Murray. Herb Stead joined me more than 25 years ago. Mr. Severson, the old Club Manager, then told me, 'You're gonna live to see this as a year 'round place.' And I said, 'Never. There's nothing here but Seminole Indians and alligators in the summer.

"We've had some celebrated people playing here, of course. Alexander Haig, George Bush, all the Fords and, of course, the Kennedys. For a while I played every day with Bobby Kennedy — that was after his brother was assassinated — and I played with Jackie. They were talking about buying a home here. Joseph Reed was a great player and a lot of fun. He had a wonderful sense of humor about it and kept it light."

Margaret Nuttle remembers:

"Joseph Reed's love of the game and of people was infectious. He was chairman of the tennis committee, and he made the whole thing go from the first day to the last. (The annual meeting was a luncheon cooked by Joseph!)

"The magnet which drew us originally to the Island was tennis as organized by Jim Pressly. His unique magnetism and humor compelled all players to play as often as possible, even beguiling them into cheerful performers in the dreaded Saturday round-robin.

"The great delight was to participate in the weekly doubles games arranged with Jim Pressly as the star player. His skill in contriving an even match and his eloquent comments on each point provided entertainment for player and spectator alike. Most notable were the morning matches with Mrs. Schuyler Van Vechten playing hearty tennis well into great-grandmotherhood and the afternoon matches with Mr. Joseph Reed who sometimes complained loudly that, 'Only on Wednesday would that man give him a day off.'

"So entertaining were Jim Pressly's commentary and Joe Reed's witty rejoinders that non-players sometimes appeared to enjoy the graceful tennis and equally graceful repartee."

More than twenty-five years later players still quote Jim Pressly. During a recent torrential downpour Jim remarked to one frustrated player that "in such weather as this I could cry unashamedly in the public market place." With Jim Pressly as Master of Court Ceremonies the question is not "Tennis, Anyone?" but "Tennis, Everyone!"

In the 1970s Joseph Reed put together a list of Jim Pressly's notable tennis-playing remarks and circulated it among the court regulars:

The Fate of Empires
or
The Game We Almost Lost

A compilation — only a small one — of the great sayings of that Captain of the Courts and that Titan of Tennis, James Pressly.

I'm going back to being inhumanly steady.
I'd rather be hit than scared to death.

Early Round Robins (left), with calls made by an umpire, were played Saturdays with Sunday finals. Today, with no umpire and many more contestants, Round Robin is a fast-paced Saturday event. On any day, members stop by the courts to watch the play (right), often before afternoon tea at the Golfhouse.

He came in on the great circle.
All organized resistance has collapsed.
Let's sail majestically through them.
They were a pale and shaken team.
The Fate of Empires hung on that shot.
Better to be lucky than good.
I'll rifle this one through the net player.
I'll give you the privilege of closing them out.
We'll give them the serve and all the modern
   advantages.
He pin-pointed his shot.
A vicious thrust.
One of the greatest lapses in modern Hobe Sound
   History.
Let's close out this always dangerous team.
He coolly picked his spot.
A moral victory not to get hit.
I can see their strategy — they're going to let us
   have the first set and then go after the next two.
Don't toy with this dangerous team.
They are bringing out our magnificent best.
How I hate a poaching net player.
They are raking our court with furious drives.
You could have driven a coach-and-four down the
   middle.
Cannily placed. Even if it hadn't been I'd have called
   it out.
It was the ease with which he did it that shook us.
Better than a good one.
A close call but a fair one.
They are delving deep into their bag of tricks.
We'll fight it out on this line all winter if necessary.

Theron Bass, Pressly's talented son-in-law, follows in Herb Stead's footsteps. Years ago, tennis shop (below) also served as golf shop.

"Dear Girl We Really <u>Must</u> Have a Garden Club"

Early Years

Lady Helen Ramsey generally is given credit for founding the Jupiter Island Garden Club. However, if I had to place a bet, I would say that one day Lady Ramsey's telephone rang and a voice said, "Dear Girl, we really must have a garden club on our Island. We must keep our ladies busy." And with those few words it all began.

The organizational meeting was held on February 22, 1952 at Lady Ramsey's. The Club's object was: "To unite its members in an active interest in the cultivation of tropical trees and plants, with the purpose of beautifying the Island and the Hobe Sound mainland." Dues were $10 per year and there were to be meetings in January, February and March. The fourteen founding members were: Admiral Sir Gordon and Lady Ramsey, Mrs. Joseph Reed, Mr. and Mrs. Ralph Hornblower, Mrs. Fred Gordon, Mrs. E. Hollie Faile, Mrs. Warner Baird, Mrs. Neil Cowham, Mrs. Carll Tucker, Mr. Jay Jacobs, Mrs. Hugo Dixon, Mrs. W.E. Oates and Mrs. Eugene Wilson.

At the Club's first meeting in January, 1953 the group took the "Palm Walk." This was a walk along the river from the Seward Johnson home to the former Beaman Davies place (now the Strohs' home). The twenty-five foot wide walk was lined on either side with Royal Palms. At intervals there were alcoves about forty feet deep. Each featured a small pool with a fountain, a piece of statuary or some art form. These centerpieces were planted with all types of flowers and shrubs, all lovely to see.

During the next four years, Club projects were the maintenance and care of the ficus trees on Bridge Road, which had been a gift of Mrs. Reed, the beautification of the railroad station on the mainland and, finally, the planting of the terrace at the Golf House. Funds were raised by Island house tours.

In 1957, after a talk by Mrs. Fergus Reid about The Garden Club of America (she had just completed her term as its President), we decided we would like to join that national organization. Proposed by the Greenwich Garden Club and seconded by the Palm Beach Garden Club, the Jupiter Island Garden Club became a member of the Garden Club of America on December 14, 1957.

by Sallie Caler

Later Years

Immediately after we were elected to membership, we learned that the 1960 Annual Meeting of the GCA was to be held in Palm Beach. Our Club was asked to entertain the delegates on the last day of the meeting — April eighth. Three hundred and eighty ladies were bussed from Palm Beach to Jupiter Island, where they toured houses and gardens, attended a flower show at the Golf House and continued on to private luncheons. It was a day to remember, with members, husbands and friends working overtime, but enjoying the effort.

Our next flower show was held in April, 1962 at the Yacht Club. Through the years, shows have been held at the Parish House, the main Clubhouse, the Beach Club and, in order to attract more people from the community, on the mainland at the Presbyterian Church. A popular exhibit at our last two shows has been a display of art, needlework, woodworking and various crafts created by Island residents. We are proud to have won the coveted Garden Club of America "Small Flower Show Award" twice.

In 1967-68 the Hobe Sound Company presented the Jupiter Island Garden Club with Harbor Island. Sallie Caler was chairman of the project that converted a wilderness into a park. A survey was made, Richard Webel donated a plan, water was piped over and hose outlets installed. The Island was cleared, leaving only desirable native plant material, and new plants were added and labeled. The lovely Japanese bridge leading from Jupiter Island attracts many visitors to this peaceful retreat. The Lady Ramsey Circle with its fountain honors our founder and first president. Sophie Richmond was in charge of the Island for many years, followed by Flossie Fort. Both have spent countless hours pruning, planting and overseeing the constant maintenance of our very special project.

In 1970, when house tours as fund-raisers were no longer practical because of security, we started our current money-raiser, the Bazaar. Permelia Reed served as chairman of the first Bazaar. It was an enourmous success and has been ever since. Held every other year under a tent next to the Parish House, the Bazaar provides the funds for our many commitments in the community.

Through the years the Club has accomplished a great deal. A top priority was the creation — and for many years the maintenance — of the walking and bicycle path known as "The Ramble." It now is so heavily used (for walking only) that it has been taken over by the Town. A lovely garden was planned and planted behind our Island Library, the ficus trees on Bridge Road have been cared for and replaced when necessary. For many years trees along A1A in Hobe Sound were planted, maintained and often replaced. Benches and trash baskets were placed at intervals along Bridge Road from the town of Hobe Sound to the Public Beach on Jupiter Island.

One of the Club's most popular and enduring projects was the brainchild of Jackson Burke in 1973. He envisioned a center on the mainland where both adults and children could learn more about their environment. After months of negotiating, the Garden Club reached an agreement with the U.S. Department of the Interior to turn an old motel on the Department's property into the Hobe Sound Nature Center. Betty Kirby and Jackson Burke worked closely in planning this project and its financing. The building was renovated, a Director was hired, programs were organized and a Board of Directors was formed. The Center now is financed by private donations, memberships, a minimal charge to summer students and a substantial donation from the Jupiter Island Garden Club. The varied programs appeal to all ages.

Recent undertakings on the mainland have been: the planting of thirty new live oak and ficus trees from the existing ficus trees to the railroad tracks, complete with a sprinkler system; providing picnic tables and benches for Zeus park (with trees to be planted in the near future); planting at the Hobe Sound Ambulance Corps' building and refurbishing the clubrooms at Banner Lake.

Scholarship aid always has been a main thrust. During the early years, teachers were sent to summer sessions at Audubon Camps. In recent years, a two-year scholarship toward college is offered every year to a Martin County High School senior who is choosing a career in one of the natural sciences. Recently the Club has received a generous, anonymous donation for scholarship aid named for, and honoring, Permelia Pryor Reed.

Martha Ashe, who served five terms as president, guiding our Club with great wisdom and talent, has served the community in yet another capacity. Every other year since 1965, she has planned and run an educational trip to some part of Florida. She has taken busloads of Islanders for an overnight or two to Everglades Park Corkscrew Swamp, Key West, Fairchild Gardens and Viscaya, to mention a few of the places.

Through the years several of our members have been recipients of Garden Club of America National Awards. In 1970, Mr. Richard Webel, one of our Honorary Members, received the Mrs. Oakleigh Thorne Medal "for his distinguished career in landscape architecture, as creator of exceptional beauty in his designs for private gardens as well as large Federal and Municipal projects."

Another Honorary Member, Mr. Nathaniel Reed, received in 1976 the Frances K. Hutchinson Medal: "A true conservationist — knowledgeable, dedicated, courageous and staunch." Both medals were presented at Annual Meetings of The Garden Club of America.

Sir John Thouron, an Island resident, has recently been elected to the prestigious group of Members at Large of The Garden Club of America.

In 1989, the Annual Meeting of The Garden Club of America will again be held in Palm Beach and the Jupiter Island Garden Club will again host a day of the meeting. We already are planning for the future and feeling secure that everyone will work to make our Island a joy to behold.

by Colt Adams

The Garden Club Bazaar occurs every other year. In 1986 it was held in this star-spangled tent erected between the Rectory and the Parish House. A regular feature of the Bazaar is the drawing for the needlepoint rug — on which chances have been sold previously — sewn by Garden Club members skilled in the craft. The 1988 rug, depicting the Signs of the Zodiac, is shown here with the ladies who did it. They are: (back row, left to right) Xenia Miller, Mary Joe Stollenwerck, Delia Blake, Thelma Moloney, Marge Ordway; (front row, left to right) Weedie Walker, Flossie Fort, Sallie Caler, Virginia Jones, Dorothy-Ray Henley. The money from the Bazaar supports the Garden Club's continuing projects: Harbor Island, Hobe Sound Nature Center, Civic Planting, Scholarships for nature-minded high school students bound for college.

Croquet Committee stands behind the center stake. From left; Phil Nuttle, Bill Strawbridge, Sealy Newell (Chairman), George Pidot. Universally, whites are required dress, hat bands optional.

Croquet

Unlike polo, which originated in Tibet and Persia in the time of Darius the Great (522-486 B.C.) with the wild tribes of Asia knocking sheep's heads about with mallets made from rocks tied to camels' shin bones and which game had become the property of kings, maharajas and real estate tycoons, very fashionable and a new venue for social climbers in Britain called "Castle Creepers", croquet originated in the chivalrous, romantic and royal courts of Languedoc in France during the 13th century. For two centuries it was a sport played almost exclusively by the rich and titled — the only ones with big backyards. Backyards became lawns; lawns became greenswards; greenskeepers were engaged. In the 1660s, in England, at least one court was made of powdered cockleshells and its wickets festooned with flowers. It was extraordinarily popular in England in the best country houses in the 17th to 19th centuries, but it now has become the property of everyone in the U.S.A., with all the hullabaloo associated with baseball, ice hockey and football. It has become so rowdy that the U.S. Croquet Association, the game's ruling body, has been forced to initiate the following rules of conduct:

1. Courtesy and sportsmanship are required. There should be no loud, abusive, profane, obscene or insulting language or gestures within the sight or sound of any other person.
2. No objects may be thrown or hit toward any other person.
3. Spectators shall refrain from audible comments on the game, may not offer advice or call attention to errors committed or about to be committed by any player. Spectators shall not abuse an official or player on pain of being ejected from the area.

As you can see, only on the lawns on Jupiter Island do chivalry, courtesy and decorum still prevail. I am indebted to John Walker, III, who started croquet on Jupiter Island, for much of the following information.

A crisis arose in England in the 1870s when some unscrupulous Irishman discovered that players were more accurate if they swung the mallet between their legs. The Women's Libbers of the day rose in furious protest. They angrily pointed out that their skirts prevented them from adopting such a style, and they compelled the United All England Croquet Association to ban "Center Play" as it was called. Only recently has the ban been remanded.

Croquet's popularity in those days is understandable. Any coed game played outdoors without chaperones would have enjoyed a certain vogue. Captain Reid in an 1863 treatise wrote that croquet was a character-building alternative to actual warfare, particulary if women could be kept away from the handsome young men who played it. In the 1860s women players wore anti-Aeolians (wire cages) to hold their skirts in trim despite winds. In that same decade the finest set of Jacques croquet equipment, eight boxwood balls, eight ivory mallets, hoops, clips, etc. and a mahogany case could be purchased for 14 pounds. Winslow Homer painted a croquet scene in 1860; it is now in the Art Institute of Chicago. When King Edward VII visited his cousin, the Kaiser of Germany, in the 1890s, he took his croquet set along.

Croquet was most popular in England and the U.S.A. between 1860 and 1900, when it was surpassed by tennis and the bicycle. However, intense interest continued as shown by a series of letters to the editor and British sports magazine in 1910. These argued the pros and cons of the decision made in 1874 to change the wickets from four inches wide to three and three-quarter inches, and to make the hoops of steel instead of wood. Only the British can work up a fury about who saw the first whippoorwill of the spring or whose hollyhocks blossomed first or the importance of a change of one quarter inch in wickets made 36 years earlier.

However, not all was roses. Bluenoses discovered that the higher virtues were not all that croquet promoted. It afforded players an ample opportunity to consume the dreaded alcohol and to gamble on the outcome of the games. A right-thinking magazine editorialized in 1898, "The game is the Gaping Jaws of Hell. It would be wise if the enthusiasm of the clergy and the laity were enlisted for suppressing the immoral practice of croquet."

In the U.S., in the 1920s, there were two main centers of croquet. One was at Herbert Bayard Swope's place at Sands Point, where Alexander Woolcott, George S. Kaufman, Dorothy Parker and Averill Harriman played frequently and exchanged argumentative, vituperative and original epithets. Mr. Harriman played actively for many years on Jupiter Island until he sold his house in 1979. He is remembered in croquet circles more for his exceptional patience, competitiveness and shooting skills than any of his many accomplishments at conference tables. On the West Coast, movie moguls Daryl Zanuck and Sam Goldwyn led Harpo Marx, Louis Jourdan, Jean Negresco, Howard and Bill Hawks, Tyrone Power, George Sanders, Gig Young and a myriad of other movie people through weekly games with bets of $10,000 on a match fairly commonplace.

As for croquet on Jupiter Island, John Walker III, a constant visitor to Britain, was familiar with croquet. He sat next to Mrs. Reed at a dinner party in 1973 and mentioned the attractions of the game to her. The next morning at nine a.m., Mrs. Reed and a bulldozer met him next to the eighth green of the golf course. A lawn was laid out, graded, seeded and in put action in the shortest possible time. That lawn, however, was moved to its present location in 1984 to make room for more tennis courts at the old location.

John Walker was for years the most dedicated and dictatorial member of the Croquet Committee — and its most active promoter — until recently when physical difficulties dictated his retiring. He gave the Walker Cup, the trophy for the winning Doubles Team. He and Mrs. Reed won this every year for 10 years. Mrs. Reed still plays actively and was runner-up in one of the tournaments in the winter of 1987.

Three tournaments are held each year, the Walker Cup Couples, the Byers Cup round robin match for teams and a singles tournament. Also, there are two one-day events a Hole-In-One contest and a medal play contest. Play is open to anyone over 18 and children over 12 if accompanied by an adult to keep them from digging into the surface.

There have been many changes over the centuries in the details and rules of the games played. At this time the standard game played all over the world is Association Croquet, a real challenge for skill and strategy. It differs from the old backyard croquet in that there are only six wickets, plus the final stake in the center of the lawn. One plays twice around the course, once clockwise, once in reverse. A player gets one stroke for going through a wicket and two extra strokes for hitting another ball, even his partner's. He cannot hit that ball again (he is dead on it) until he gets through another wicket. You can knock another ball a distance if you put your ball against it, but you cannot put your foot on your ball to hold it in place. A great part of the tactics is to keep your ball away from your opponents' so they cannot play off it even if you have to go out of bounds. Teamwork between partners is essential.

by Sealy Newell

Bridge

Pierre Houdry likes to recall the time Police Chief Warwick was cruising slowly down Beach Road when a car driven by Pierre's Mother shot by at high speed. Lights flashing and sirens blowing, the Chief pulled the driver over and growled, "Where's the fire?"

"It's at the Dolans'," Mrs. Houdry shot back, "and I'm late for my bridge!"

From the very beginning, the Jupiter Island Club has held the game of bridge in high esteem. There is at least one enthusiast in almost every family.

Polly Dolan, until her death in 1981, was considered the best bridge player on the Island. She firmly believed that bridge provides a fascinating hobby for people as they grow older and are unable to participate in active sports. She was dedicated and she brooked no nonsense. Players were supposed to use every brain cell and she minced few words in drawing her partner's attention to mistakes. Nevertheless, she was admired and loved by all.

Mrs. Dolan's daughter, Peggy Miller, remembers her Mother's afternoon foursomes. Concentration was absolute. If Peggy wanted to serve ice water — the sole beverage permitted during the game — she would enter the room only when the cards were being shuffled.

She has a vivid recollection of her Mother saying to her, after she had made an error, "Once the bidding is completed, you have no excuse for not knowing the cards in every hand!"

In the 1950s Boris Koytchou, a champion player with a charming personality, was asked to spend six weeks at the Club each year, giving classes and private lessons. The interest in bridge increased so much that Permelia Reed

and Boris thought it would add to everyone's enjoyment if there were an annual match with the Everglades Club of Palm Beach. Each Club would enter an eight-man team; the match would be held one year on Jupiter Island, the next in Palm Beach. The Everglades Club was delighted with the idea, and the matches began.

The first Jupiter Island team included Polly Dolan, Fifi Dorrance Colket, another excellent player, Mathilde Shea (Kernan), Marie Bartlett, Rachel and Petrus Meyeringh (Island Club President for the years 1953-59) and Permelia Reed. Mrs. Reed presented a cup, which went back and forth. In the 1970s Col. Weedin, a member of the Everglades Club, presented another cup, this for a second team of twelve. This naturally generated even more interest in making a team. Among the players are two delightful Canadian women, Fran Allen and Clayton Burton, who spend part of the winter at the Club, The Hon. Douglas Dillon, Billy and Donald Agnew, Frannie Fentress, Glad Scheerer and many others. Bettie Ely always took part until her death.

Jupiter Island-Everglades matches were of utmost importance to Polly Dolan. She never willingly missed a tournament. But once she had to. She underwent a serious operation on the day of the match. When she came out of the anesthetic, her first words to her daugher were: "Who won?"

For some years bridge lessons were given in January and February. But as interest in bridge continued to grow, it was decided to have an additional six lessons starting in November. Bill Root, a 6'8" world-champion player, took the assignment, and his popularity increases each year.

After twenty-five years of teaching on Jupiter Island, Boris Koytchou decided to retire. To take his place he suggested Alan Truscott, a syndicated bridge columnist for the *New York Times* and many other newspapers. A personable man with a great sense of humor, Truscott has written several books on the game, as has his wife Dorothy Hayden. He is a delight to have on the Island — an ardent tennis player and jogger and ready to entertain at the drop of a hat by singing Gilbert and Sullivan.

Truscott gives three classes each week: intermediate, refresher and Saturday morning's duplicate practice for players interested in team play. The program runs smoothly, thanks to the efforts of the Chairman of the Bridge Committee, first Billy Agnew, then Colt Adams and now Zosia Rogers.

The annual Polly Dolan Tournament, the equivalent of a Club championship, is now a high spot of the bridge year. John and Atheline Wilbur won the first tournament, George and Jane Offutt won the second, and, after George's untimely death, Jane Offutt and Peggy Williams won the third.

Some years ago Admiral Richard Tuggle and his wife Elizabeth started afternoon bridge — in the winter at the Golf House, in the summer at the Beach Club. There are usually two or three tables — low stakes, Chicago bridge, mixed expertise. Anyone wishing a game drops in, checks on a table, indicating a desire to cut in, and takes the place of the first person to cut out. These games are popular both with Island residents and Club guests.

Although the life of Hobe Sound encompasses many interests, bridge players always find themselves happily busy with friends who share their love of the game.

by Billie Agnew

Still-lifes, Landscapes, and a Paucity of Nudes

by Colby Chester

Inside the Parish House, April 1987, visitors at the annual one-day exhibition view the chez d'oeuvres. Here one can buy the "perfect" painting for $80 to $500.

The Jupiter Island Art Class was formed in 1968, and from the start it attracted lots of Island talent — some beginning, some experienced and all congenially dedicated. For two years the Class met in a building, south of the golf practice range, better known as "The Barn" which was anything other than ideal as a studio being hot, dark and cluttered with attic treasures for the biennial Garden Club Bazaar. It made a deal with Christ Memorial Church to use the Parish House where, contentedly, it still holds its classes. The teacher was Robert (Robbie) Merletto who lived on Jupiter Island and worked for the Norton Gallery in West Palm Beach. The author begins his narrative in 1971 when he and his wife, Jane, became residents of the Island.

Shortly after Jane and I moved to Jupiter Island we were invited to Bettie and Reds Ely's for dinner. Bettie and I had painted together many times in the past when we all summered at Fishers Island, and I knew that this dinner invitation was primarily to tell me about the Jupiter Island Art Class and to persuade me to join up. Bettie, it turned out, had great respect for Robbie Merletto and thought that he was one of the finest teachers she had ever known. I didn't have to be persuaded.

After dinner, Reds and I retired to his den, and he told me that even he who had never painted in his life had joined the Class for the 1970-71 season and thought it was great. In fact, he then told me about their first "Art Show" put on that season. He said it was held off the Island somewhere up in the Stuart area and that Robbie had brought a friend from the Norton Gallery to judge it. Everyone in the Class had an entry. Reds had completed, as far as I could make out, only one painting the whole year, and it was of a rooster, which was his entry (a Rhode Island Red I am sure). "Guess what painting was awarded 'Best in Show'?" Reds said. "I wouldn't dare guess," I replied. "Why it was the Rooster," he preened.

Reds never came back to the Class after his victorious year. I probed him some more about Robbie, for some other friends had told me that he was pretty rough on some of the members, and he had turned them off completely. But Reds quickly rose to Robbie's defense. It seems that after a few sessions many of the classmates complained

that although Robbie prepared many fine still lifes for their weekly subject boredom set in, and they clamored for something more exciting to paint. Robbie agreed that he would do what he could to improve matters. Two weeks later the Class assembled. From the wings Robbie led in a young lady, flicked off her serape and there stood a lovely nude! Not all the men were in the class that day but, in short order, one who had slipped out rounded up the stragglers and the class got underway in full swing. I do not know whether or not Robbie was reprehended for this bold diversion, but I do know I have never had another chance to paint a real live nude in all the sixteen years I've painted on Jupiter Island.

Hank Flower, a founding father of the Class, also painted once a week in a class in Tequesta. Every Tuesday (the day we met for our Class) Hank would bring in a painting he had done in Tequesta to get Robbie's critique on it because, Hank said, the teacher in Tequesta never gave critiques and he valued Robbie's immensely.

One day Hank came in with a painting of a beautiful brunette lolling on a chaise lounge. The whole class was astonished, for Hank had never painted a picture of this type, and it clearly was not painted in his style. Hank invariably painted sea and landscapes in a somewhat heavy-handed style — but they were good. That day the Class reverted to a debating forum — the few pros congratulating Hank on a marvelous painting, the cons accusing him of bringing in a sample of his Tequesta teacher's work — a sheer plagiarism. Hank stuck to his guns and insisted it was his. The Class was in a frenzy and soon broke up.

It was not 'till about two years later over cocktails at his house that Hank admitted to me that the painting was done by a young girl in his Tequesta class and he had brought it to Jupiter Island, not to claim it as his own, but to persuade us to go to Tequesta to see her work and possibly buy one of her paintings if we were so minded. However, things got so out of hand so quickly that he never had a chance to get the true story across!

Merletto was an interesting teacher. Although he was basically a sculptor and not a painter, his critiques of his students' paintings at the end of each Class were excellent — brief, inspiring and to the point. He was temperamental, especially towards beginners and new members of the class who were already accomplished painters. For the first three or four lesson periods his critiques often were denigrating, often producing tears and, in more than one case, the recipient of his remarks quit the class. On the other hand, if one "bit the bullet", in due time Robbie would all but dote over him (or her), praising his work, assuring him he had true talent and perserverance would take him far!

By 1980, the Class had grown to 24 people and was divided into three sections — Monday afternoons, Tuesday, and Saturday mornings. There were now six males in the Class (today only two) and feeling they could not forego Monday golf for a painting class opted for Tuesday morning instead. Five ladies who no longer could put up with Merletto's temperament formed a Class of their own for Fridays and hired an instructor more to their liking from Tequesta. That was the status from 1980 to 1982.

From the mid '70s on, Bill Harris had become the Committee Chairman of the Class. His was not an easy job, but he handled it magnificently. He dealt with the parish and our use of the premises; he hired the personnel to do the cleaning; he arranged our contract with Merletto each year and acted as arbiter in all the disputes between members of the Class and Robbie; he kept the Class going for several years each time Merletto threatened to quit. But the time came when even Bill Harris could not work his magic. At the end of the 1982 season, Merletto gave us his final notice. Previously he had sold his house on Jupiter Island and had gone to Guatemala for the summer where he bought some property and started to build a house. It was not complete, and he returned to Stuart and reluctantly agreed to instruct the Class that year, 1980-81. That summer more or less the same thing happened — the Guatemala house not completed, Robbie was back that fall to conduct his last Class.

By the early '80s there were many newcomers to Jupiter Island — several of whom joined the Art Class. When we learned for certain that Merletto was not coming back, many meetings were held to determine what could be done to keep the Class going. Most of the old timers who had often said that they would drop out if Robbie was not the instructor threatened to do so, and a few did. Most of the newcomers, however, said the Class must continue come what may.

Bettie Ely took over from Bill Harris and started a drive to find someone in the environs who could replace Merletto. It was a difficult task. Finally, a young man by the name of Tom Lohr was hired for the job. He was primarily a portraitist, but seemed happy and willing to contend with us. It seemed he was a good artist in his chosen field, but really too young and unsophisticated to demonstrate his talents or properly convey his lore adequately to this elderly group. During his second season he brought many of his own paintings to the studio and seemed to spend more time trying to sell his works than instructing the Class. Everyone agreed that Lohr would have to go.

Bettie Ely passed her Chairmanship of the Committee over to Weedie Walker who reluctantly agreed to take over and do her best to find a person to fill the bill. This was accomplished in a few short weeks. Christopher Starvos, a fine artist who lives in Hobe Sound in the winters and Maine in the summers and runs a rather large Class among mainland Hobe Sound residents, agreed to come to the Island three days a week. His tenure began in November of 1984 and continues now. We still have an "Art Show" at the end of each season.

Weedie Walker (with Katie Greeff as Treasurer), having done so much in re-establishing the Class on a sound basis, has turned the baton over to Honor Seaman, with Katie still as Treasurer. Over the years the size of the Class has grown and ebbed, but it has never been below 20. The coming years promise to be good ones. Many new people have expressed their desire to join us. I hope they do. There can be no greater feeling of selflessness, timelessness and purpose than to sit (or stand) at an easel, palette in hand, and let one's emotions produce (good, bad, or indifferent) one's own creation.

The last two survivors of what was once a respectably sized bevy of male artists take a respite from Tuesday's class on the steps of the Parish House. The author is at left; at right, Don Richardson.

"Corsair," originally built and owned by Harry Corse, designer of
21 Island houses, is home of Permelia Reed who enlarged it.

Two of the five earliest houses were Coconut Point (above) and the Snider/Wares/Holton/Kessler "fishing camp" (below). A cottage when Captain Armour built it in 1886, Coconut Point was owned subsequently by Dawes/Kirby/Stroh. Kessler home was renovated recently but kept its original character.

Island Homes and ...

by Tom Green

The construction of the first substantial building on Jupiter Island in 1859, the lighthouse, was halted not by budgetary difficulties or labor disputes, but by Seminole arrows. During the ensuing 30 years, there were, perhaps, 12 fishing shacks along the shore of the snaking river that cut Jupiter Island from the mainland. It was not until the 1890s that five houses, then referred to as "fishing camps," were built within a few years of each other and within the general area of the present "S" curve. One of these was Coconut Point, home of Captain James A. Armour who boated down river to tend to the lighthouse. Another was the house the Yates family built on the west side of the Fork (now the Bridges' house) with materials waded across the river. The wild growth, thick and wet at the river's edge, swarmed with chiggers and mosquitoes.

From an architectural standpoint there was nothing notable in these early houses. They were simple, large and comfortable with exposed rafter ends and little attempt at ornamentation except for the prevalence of interior columns which may have been necessitated by alteration or addition and not a part of original design. That these first houses were considered to be merely "fishing camps" belied their size and appearance. In his fishing camp (the Van Fleet/McChristian house) Mr. Joseph Jefferson entertained President Grover Cleveland. Further, he installed German landscape architect, Fred Schultz, in the gardener's cottage (now the enlarged Lind house) to create the magnificent alées and gardens with their

Caler house, 1910, was first house with flare on the Island.

...the Rewards of Diversity

Architect Jane Doggett's Persian home, oceanfront in the '80s.

punctuation of statuary and fountains. Thus, a Sunday stroll — parasol and chiffon — a "fishing camp" afternoon.

In the same vein and during the same years, Major Eugene C. Lewis, President of the Louisville Nashville Railroad, built his log cabin lined with cedar shipped down from Nashville. It stood just south of the "S" curve on the highest ridge on the Island. He had ordered an orange grove to be shipped by barge. When he saw this forest moving upon him, he promptly thought of *Macbeth* and named his place Dunsinane. On the front door of Dunsinane the Major hung a sign which read: "No Dogs, No Cats, No Suffragettes."

In 1916, Mr. William Angas, the representative of the Land Mortgage Co. of Yorkshire, England, built a small inn and three cottages. Architecturally, Mr. Angas followed the precepts set back in the 1890s — simplicity and function. However, some of the houses at this time were more elaborate. With its cornices and columned portico, the Pitou/Murphy/Caler house, built in 1910, stood as the precursor of future attention to design, detail and embellishment. The five Bassett houses, built in a row on the north end of Gomez Road in 1925, are interesting examples of the change of attitude toward Island homes. Although the principal reason for the Bassetts leaving Palm Beach was fishing, their houses were hardly "fishing camps" even in the Island lexicon. From the early '30s on, the expansion of the Jupiter Island Club's facilities brought a change of attitude toward the Island's offerings.

Distinct Japanese influence appears in the William Moore house.

McMahon house, mid-'80s, shows the prevalent Bermuda style.

Geer/Voorhees/Nash/Traphagen is a Spanish-inspired '20s house.

Meandering Spanish compound of the Barry and Bridges families.

The Benington house is one of Harry Corse's Art Deco works.

Contemporary Miller house has roofless pool within its confines.

Lind house was actor Joseph Jefferson's caretaker's cottage.

On his arrival in 1916, William Angas became the Island's first builder. He built the clubhouse (at top), as well as three guest cottages, of which Hibiscus (middle) and Sea Grape (bottom) are pictured here. The simple, straightforward style of architecture which Angas employed set the tone for all of the buildings of the Jupiter Island Club erected in later years.

Johnson house, architect Kemp Caler's Island masterpeice, is a recreation of a New York Yacht Club boathouse shore station.

Fishing became less of a primary lure while golf, tennis, beach life, social gatherings and community activities came to the forefront.

Today's Jupiter Island with its 430 houses, full Club facilities and unique landscaping is to a great extent the reflection of four influences. Quite unlike other clubs or planned developments which generally insist on a single architectural style, Jupiter Island contains a remarkable diversity which resulted, not by accident, but from policy. In 1931 there were 28 houses on the Island, six of which were owned by the Club; thus, a particular architectural precedent or style had not been established. Two years later when Mr. Joseph Verner Reed took over the Hobe Sound Company, his philosophy was that nice people would build nice houses, and his dictum was that residents should not be held to restrictions of design and style.

The Town of Jupiter Island later passed ordinances governing zoning, siting, maximum heights, minimum square footage of houses and amount of lot coverage. But architectural self-expression became the rule, and it most certainly has flourished. One very large new house on the Island even has a free form, bridged, indoor pond replete with waterfalls, lighting and sound system that can carry a dinner guest through a sunset's glow to the light of a rising moon to the gathering and smash of a thunderstorm so perfectly that one worries about open car windows. That is diversity.

For about two decades new construction revealed a surprising variety of architectural influences: Spanish, Japanese, South African and the popular Bermudan. At the root of

Its unusual frosting decorates one of the largest parcels of land on Jupiter Island, with 600 feet fronting on the Intracoastal.

this multiplicity stood the would-be homeowners with their incomplete plans, the three or more builders with a knowledge of the Island and several sets of acceptable plans, the designer with five or six layouts that could be interchanged or modified. Then there were the architects. Florida law governing domestic architecture does not require the services of an architect. The local building inspector rules under the Southern States Building Code and local ordinances. Consequently, both the amateurs and the professionals left their stamp.

In the mid-thirties two such men with a shared interest in building came to the Island, and they make an interesting comparison. Both Architect Harry Corse and Dr. George St. John, headmaster of his Choate School, held a keen appreciation of the Island. Mr. Corse built 21 houses, the schoolhouse and much of the Beach Club and locker rooms. Some of his homes do not bear his stamp but on others — mostly on the ocean — he did leave his unmistakable mark. It was he who, somewhat late, evoked that era of short, sequined dresses, the Charleston and the Tiffany lamps with houses in Art Deco style. Emphasis was placed on the stark relationship of vertical to horizontal plane, a composition of wall blocks of various sizes, devoid of curve or angle and relieved by an unexpected use of glass block. Although Mrs. Kelley worked on the design of her house with Mr. Corse and terms it Roman, it bears a distinct kinship with such period pieces as those of Hatch, Benington, Bourassa, Stewart and Mellon.

On the very first day he ever set foot on Jupiter Island, Dr. George St. John bought a piece of property on it. A year later he began to enjoy his favorite pastime, building houses;

J.D. Bassett, the forefather of the large Virginia clan on the Island, moved from Palm Beach in 1925 for the fishing. His house (bottom) was later sold to M.D. Grant, but the four houses he built for his children remain in the family including the Vaughan (top) and Leisy (middle) houses, both radical departures from the prevalent beach-houses architectural style.

81

not for others as did Mr. Corse, but for himself and family with a weather eye on selling in the future. His fascination with the Island centered about its beauty, on his ocean-to-river stretch of property, its views of land and sea. Further, it is apparent that he believed a winter retreat should be simple and maintenance-free. One finds, therefore, lightly stained cypress beach houses with all rooms opening to patio, sea grape and ocean beachfront. Rental of the first house during months when Choate was in session encouraged acquisition of additional property and construction of another house. The sale of one meant construction of a third over on that site with such a fine view. For thirty-odd years and eight houses, so it went. Of Dr. St. John's eight houses, seven still stand with one, "Jetsam," remaining in the family.

Exceptionally lovely settings for beautiful homes and the willingness of wealthy homeowners to pay for them plus freedom from design restrictions were a golden opportunity for architects. Burrall Hoffman designed his own house overlooking the golf course, and Mr. and Mrs. Koming Prosser were so enchanted by it that they asked the architect to duplicate it for them on an adjacent lot. And so he did insofar as the floor plan; however, he gave the house an English Regency facade, thus creating two distinctively different homes. In an enlarged version with a better flow Mr. Hoffman did reproduce his own house on the site of Dunsinane, a work of restrained elegance. In the same vein he built the Dillon house with an exterior reminiscent of his own and an interior of meticulous detail that rivals any on the Island.

Kemp Caler moved to the Island in the forties and began to practice his art as an architect both in Palm Beach and Jupiter Island. In his years on the Island, Mr. Caler has built the astonishing number of 50 houses. His work is distinctive Caler; traditional approach with unusual attention paid to unexpected custom features. The effort of which Mr. Caler is most proud is the Johnson boathouse, his stunning recreation of the old New York Yacht Club shore station. With its diamond-paned casement windows, French doors and wonderful jig-saw tracery festooning the building and all shining white against the brown shingled walls and roof, the composition evokes the whimsical delight of a giant gingerbread house. The three other houses on Mr. Caler's list of particular favorites are those of C. Runnells, J. Simpson and H.U. Harris, as well as they might be.

During the '20s and early '30s the Mediterranean Revival, the architectural style which Addison Mizner espoused to transform the face of Palm Beach, made its appearance on Jupiter Island. Addison Mizner himself never built a house here, but his followers built several. A Palm Beach architect named Maurice Fatio (pronounced Fat-see-oh) erected a home on Gomez Road now owned by Dominick. He built Artemis, a grand, two-story villa, spacious yet warm and inviting in the Mediterranean style with its loggia facing west and its terrace of multi-shaped stone stretching toward the river. This was the Reeds' home during the '30s (photo, p. 36) until the move to Corsair at wartime when Joseph joined the Army and Permelia took charge of the Inn. Later, it was torn down to make way for the Marshall Field house. Fatio also put up the little hacienda next to the Huber property and pressed on with his Mediterranean Revival into the arms of the Fork — now the handsome Murray house, enlarged and restored. At about the same time a West Palm Beach architect, L. Phillips Clark, built a house on Links Road which, after decades of ownership by the Voorhees family and a brief oc-

cupancy by the Nashes, was bought and restored by its current owners, the Traphagens. Its tower and and lover's staircase are delightful Mediterranean elements. In 1930, Mrs. William Barstow decided to build a beach house for entertaining. Palm Beach architects irritated her; she thought they were snobs. So she prevailed upon her husband to look further afield. He engaged the firm of Marsh and Saxelbye in Jacksonville who created, in the Mizner style, the house which was bought, restored and enlarged by the Offutts in 1960. Its living room, lofty in scale, is perfect for distinctive entertaining. The great stone fireplace and the opposing arched view of ocean beyond stone terrace are masterful strokes, and the high storied, coffered, painting ceiling imparts the whole with an aura of other places, other times.

So ranges the architectural diversity of the Island; however, it cannot be noted by the Sunday driver. Perhaps the greatest, single influence in transforming Jupiter Island into a visual delight was that of Mr. and Mrs. Richard Webel who made landscaping an integral part of its architecture. From Mrs. Reed's *A Kaleidoscope of Jupiter Island:* "The roads around the Club, the parking lots, the redesign of the patios, the area around the Beach Club, the last nine holes of the golf course, and so much else, we owe to his genius." It was not, however, merely Club property on which the Webel talent was exercised. Having worked extensively in the New York environs for many people with winter homes on the Island, quite naturally the Webels were again called upon. So popular did their form of landscaping become that one was said to have Webelized his property.

In a sense theirs was rather Japanese in approach with vestiges of a clipped, English formality in that the whole was gradually revealed in a series of surprises. Thus, there came the curving driveway with its high hedging and clumps of planting in varying, almost layered heights obscuring the house until the final swing to courtyard or circle. To create a final surprise, any view of what lay beyond the house was usually planted out with first sight of lawn and waterway or ocean reserved for living room or terrace. On the sides of the property, Mr. Webel used hedges or carefully placed plantings, not an original idea but always artfully done, to make one unaware of neighbors. On smaller, interior lots, Mr. Webel used the same overall concept but reduced the scale. Again there was the curved driveway and the protective planting, and the area to the rear treated as though it were a secret garden with, perhaps, a fountain or pool.

In such a way, Mr. Richard Webel gave and continues to give Jupiter Island much of its unique quality — seclusion, tranquility and an ordered design that fits into the natural environ. It is due to him and to the standards of architecture that have come to pass here that we are spared the sight of pretentious columns or baroque facades or blatantly ornate statue-cornered terraces all gleaming nakedly in the sun. And it is due to Joseph Verner Reed that we are spared having to gaze upon home after home cut from the same tiresome mold.

Mrs. George Offutt's living room. Built by William Barstow in 1930 of Island-quarried coquina stone, the house was purchased, enlarged and restored by the Offutts in 1960. The finest example of the Mediterranean Revival style on Jupiter Island has always been this room with its grand proportions and coffered ceiling still decorated in original paint.

Tales of the Yacht Club
Rip Van Winkle and Friends

by Seymour St. John

1892, barely beyond memory. The Island is covered with low scrub. Only a ficus or rubber tree here and there pokes up its head. Mosquito-breeding mangroves line the river front, while to the east along the ocean stretches a broad and pristine beach. It all looks as it did to the Hoe Bay Indians, and in 1696, to Jonathan Dickinson. The casuarinas will not show up for two decades. The Florida East Coast track is not yet laid through Hobe Sound. The Celestial Railroad, eight miles of it, connects the boat docks of Jupiter and Juno. All else is water transport. There will be no bridge to the mainland for another 19 years. The paddle wheel steamboat has just begun chugging its route from the railhead at Titusville to Jupiter. There are a few dwellings on the Island but there is no drinking water, no electricity, no road. Boats are the way of life, a pleasure and a necessity. Sailing the river, both settlers and visiting sportsmen need support, partly to provide community docks and supply centers, partly for companionship in this lonely wilderness. So, the Hobe Sound Yacht Club has its beginning when the little group of men first gather together on St. Patrick's Day, 1892.

Yacht Club records before 1915 are sparse. But we do know that on that 17th day of March the popular thespian, Joe Jefferson, was elected first Commodore. Best known for his performance of Rip Van Winkle, Joe played across the country and indeed the world. According to a Palm Beach journal of the '90s, "February 20th, natal day of Joe Jefferson was always the occasion of a Club luncheon at 'the Garden of Eden.'" These luncheons were such famously sumptuous stag events, lasting until dusk, that the local newspapers published the menus which on one occasion included pate of lark's liver in aspic! The host invariably toasted Joe Jefferson who invariably responded with wit; and at the last, everyone arose and joined in wishing the grand old actor would "live long and prosper" — Rip Van Winkle's toast.

Jefferson brought to his fishing camp on the Island an interesting group of theater people: from playwright, Joe Arthur, to actress, Fanny Brice, to producers, Charles Osgood and Augustus Pitou. Story has it that he also invited more seductive members of the cast to stay at one of the Island homes built at the turn of the century. His best-known guest (as has been noted in a previous article) was President Grover Cleveland, who, like Jefferson, was an avid fisherman.

Jefferson's humour ranged widely. When he went surf-casting he was naturally arrayed, not as the lilies of the field, but in the disreputable garments every good fisherman wears.

First Commodore was Joe Jefferson, Rip Van Winkle of the stage.

Walking the beach one morning he encountered two twittering tourists.

"Oh, I know who you are; you are Alligator Joe," chirped one, referring to a character who kept an alligator farm up the Loxahatchee.

"Madam," responded Jefferson, bowing and doffing a battered hat, "I admit the Joe but deny the Alligator."

Another story that warmly touches our first Commodore: on a cold December day in 1870 he visited his New York church asking that the rector conduct the funeral service of his friend, George Holland, who had died the previous day. On learning that Holland was an actor, the rector refused to have such a funeral solemnized in his church. Astonished and hurt, Jefferson asked where he could go on behalf of his friend. The rector replied that there was "a little church around the corner where they do that sort of thing."

"God bless the little church around the corner," said Jefferson. And to this day the Church of the Atonement on 29th Street has been so remembered. A stained glass window memorializes the moment; and the tune to Jefferson's words became the hit of the 1870s.

During the first 20 years of growing Island habitation all houses were built facing the river, and all had "water gates" where small boats could land their passengers, and docks where trade boats could bring in supplies. The Yacht Club was the center of social life. There was no Clubhouse, but "it was the custom for all Club members to sail on the Sound on Sunday and to gather at the home of one of the members for high tea late in the afternoon. Club dues were $5.00." And in 1917 the Yacht Club, one of the first three in Florida, received its official stamp of approval when it adopted a burgee and was registered in Lloyd's.

After the Florida East Coast Railroad reached the village of Hobe Sound in 1895, a narrow gauge siding was laid from the Hobe Sound station to a dock on the west side of the river. In a hand-drawn cart on the rails one trundled luggage, supplies, water and ice — precious ice — from depot to river pier, thence by boat home. One had to count on losing a fair proportion of that last commodity in the tropical heat. But enough remained for the home ice chest to give some small staying power to milk, butter and perishables. Jupiter was another port of call on the river's west bank. Year-round families like the Hildebrands would sputter down the river each morning to take their children to school there.

Just about every family that bought land and built a house on the Island in those early days produced an officer of the Yacht Club. William Angas was Vice Commodore from 1915 to 1922. Newton Banner, one of the giants of the Hobe Sound mainland community after whom Banner Lake was named, was Treasurer from 1915 to 1919. J.H. Grant, who arrived from England in 1886, was Fleet Captain until 1924. Knowledgeable about boats, the first called in an emergency, he served as superintendent of Jupiter Island properties for their owners. From 1896 to 1901 he and his family lived in the Charles Jackson House, Surfside, the first dwelling built on the Island. Mrs. Grant started and ran the first inn of mainland Hobe Sound, the Wigwam.

Captain Armour's house, Coconut Point, the Island's second dwelling, might have been named more appropriately "The Commodore's Barge." Three of its four owners from 1916 to 1969 were Commodores: T.H. Allen, Beman Dawes and Captain Leonard Kirby. A charter Yacht Club member and close friend of Joe Jefferson was Fred Yates, who, in 1894, built the charming Spanish-style, tile-roofed house now owned by the Bridges. It was Yates' huge caretaker, Titus "Tiny" Hart, who 20 years later, planted and kept watering the casuarinas which were to become such a hallmark of the Island. And it was the Yates' donkey that hauled the huge barrel of water up and down the Island for that purpose.

The social activities of the Yacht Club came to a high point under the command of Commodore Ned Murphy (1923-1932) and continued in the same lively vein under Commodore William Barstow who succeeded him. By this time the Club had the use of a clubhouse — a room in Riverview cottage loaned by the Hobe Sound Company — with a long north-south dock where the Jupiter Island Club dock now stands. The Murphys bought Isle Ridge, the home built by the Club's second Commodore, Augustus Pitou.

Not surprisingly, the man named Murphy made the most of St. Patrick's Day. It started off with a party at Isle Ridge. Then, writes a later Commodore, Ralph Roosevelt, "all boarded the waiting yachts to take part in the cruise to Sunrise Inn in Stuart. Many yachts from Palm Beach and more distant places assembled at the Club and took part in the

The Lucius Robinsons (c. 1920s) enjoy a spin on the river.

manoeuvers, which were colorful and sometimes led by a band." According to Marcelle Hildebrand, who frequented these parties, "Commodore Murphy was on a strict diet...but ate masses of ham, was not allowed strong liquors but overlooked that in honor of St. Patrick." Mrs. Murphy was a lively little lady who invariably wore a hat indoors and out and sported white gloves and a parasol. Her great step-niece, Peggy Spencer St. John, held that the hat was essential to keep her wig straight.

Buying Florida real estate in that time of endless uninhabited shoreline with little or no support or protection was a dicey game. But to the snowbelt dwellers it looked like heaven. Joe Jefferson's house has disappeared, but the fine house he built in 1902 for his son Charles still stands. The manner in which this house was purchased is an interesting example of how some people landed here. In 1912 the Lucius Robinsons from frigid Rochester, New York, were headed south on their boat, *Dolly de Moss,* considering the purchase of property in the Palm Beach area. As they churned down the Indian River, their propeller became snarled in a fish seine, and they were forced to come ashore to disentangle it. The nearest dock chanced to be that of Charles Jefferson. So enchanted was the family with this strip of paradise that Mrs. Robinson asked, "Why go further?" And ascertaining that the gem was for sale, they bought it on the spot. Robinson not only went on to the office of Vice Commodore from 1915 to 1932, but added the neighboring Snider property for his daughter's family, the Fred Gordons.

By the mid-1920s the north and south bridges to the mainland had been built and roads put through — the beginning of the end of boating life as a necessity. Automobiles came in, and the Yacht Club role as center of Island life diminished. In the 1940s under Commodore Archie Roosevelt the Club took one more nautical fling with Wood Pussy races. But the hurricane of '49 finished that enterprise; the borrowed clubhouse reverted to its owner and in 1954 the Club moved to its present location — sans dock.

Once again, as with Christ Memorial Chapel, Mrs. William Barstow came to the fore. Her gift of the land on the river enabled the Club to put up a modest building where cookouts and simple social functions could be held. The facilities grew as the Club became popular for its dinners and for special parties. It has also been host to the Whiz Kids since they started meeting 20 years ago. Founded by Charles Dewey and George Ketchum as a means of getting husbands out of the house for lunch, this group holds convivial Wednesday collations with a variety of speakers ranging from Edward Teller to James Michener, Douglas Dillon to Dennis Connor. No minutes or accounts are kept; no bylaws or regs are followed; no officers are elected. The membership is limited to the number who can sit at a single table. The only absolute: adjourn in time for afternoon golf.

Membership has jumped from the original dozen to 175. The list of yachts has included many kinds and sizes of craft from the 80-foot *Exact* owned by Burr Bartram former Commodore, New York Yacht Club, down to a nine-foot sloop. The hazard of the boom swinging across in a jibe doubtless accounted for the latter's name, *Head Shrinker.*

The present Yacht Club without yachts would seem to be an anomaly. But nautical tradition still flies as high as the Club burgee, which, in 1987, was duly and ceremoniously raised as it is each year. Dressed in Yacht Club pocketed blazers, ties and whites, Commodores and Governors stroll down the lawn to the flag pole, grasp the halyards to send aloft the ensign, burgee and Commodore's flag. To one Governor is entrusted the lanyard to fire the cannon announcing the opening of the season. At the appointed moment of 12:30 hours, flags are hoisted, lanyard pulled. But hold — what aberration is this? No sound forthcoming. Another yank. Continued silence. The gunnery officer leans forward, adjusts the charge in the breech, tests the firing pin, and...BOOM!...the blast blows the cannoneer back in a cloud of smoke. But tradition has held. It probably happened to Admiral Farragut in his day. So it's damn the torpedoes; full speed ahead. And may the Yacht Club "live long and prosper."

When, in 1912, the Robinsons came down river in their boat, *Dolly de Moss* — piloted by a properly uniformed crew — and put in by accident at Charles Jefferson's watergate (now the McChristian place), they saw the vision: lawn carved out of the jungle, lethal cactus replaced by fruit trees, coconut palms, bananas, hibiscus, live oak hung with Spanish moss, a tradeboat idling along offshore, a dock where the children could play with their gaff-rigged sloops. The vision has lasted for 75 years.

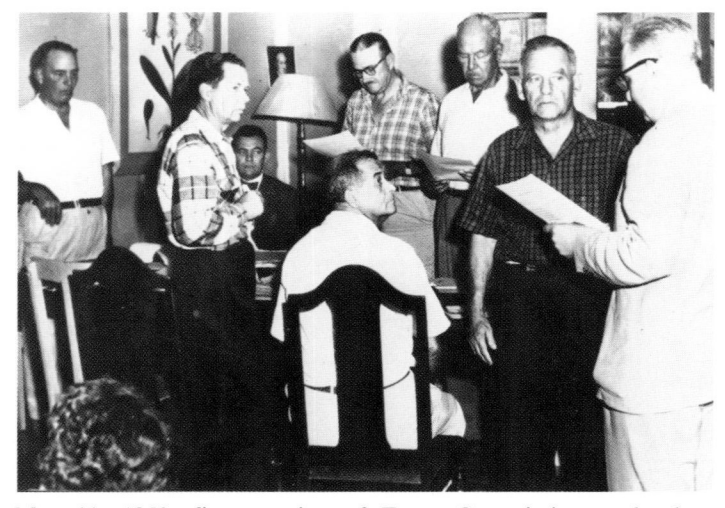

May 11, 1953: first meeting of Town Commission took place in Murphy building, former Army barracks. Mayor Griscom Bettle, second from right, and the four other Commissioners listen to the Town attorney. Seated is Admiral Richard Tuggle, first Town Manager. Present Town Hall (right) is dedicated to Permelia and Joseph Reed; the sundial to Mayor Gordon Lamont.

April 6, 1987: first woman Commissioner, Peggy Cole, is sworn in by Martin County Judge David Harper. Other Commissioners taking oath are Hugo Rutherfurd (center) for second term and Tom Green for his first. In photo directly above are the Sixth Mayor, John Mulliken, (right) who served on Commission for six years, and the current Mayor, Oliver Havens.

New Town, Less Sand, More People

by John Mulliken

In 1944, the tiny population of Jupiter Island was exactly 75 residents. During the next nine years it jumped to 140 of whom half owned houses on the ocean front. In the face of this rate of growth, which was more likely to speed up than diminish, the residents decided that three things must come to pass to protect themselves and their properties: more police; local powers of zoning and taxation; curb the erosion of the beach.

At the time, Jupiter Island was an unincorporated area on the Martin County map, administered by the Commissioners in Stuart. A Resident's Association was in place, an overseeing body that kept an eye on the condition of the roads, owned a firehouse on Bunker Hill Road, a fire

In 1985 the Town Hall had to be enlarged, but it kept its style: garage for two fire trucks; police station with a fine office for the Chief, one for the lieutenant, interrogation rooms; large entrance hall; reception desk for the dispatchers; kitchenette and dining space for lunches, snacks, staff meetings; and finally, after many patient years, separate toilets for men and women. The Town Hall wing stayed the same except for one notable addition. This was a gift from Bobsy and Pete Wick (the fifth Mayor), a handsome, properly furnished office for the Mayor. Previously, the only private quarters where His Honor could work was in his own home or in the Town Manager's office which he borrowed occasionally, or at a tiny table tucked away in the corner of the public meeting room. Often he could be found there — rather pitifully, one thought — crouched over his telephone notes.

Innumerable minor matters come before the Town government ranging from a squabble about the location of a hedge between two houses to a complaint that somebody's roadside water sprinkler has been dousing passing cars. But the two major issues that worry it the most are beach erosion and the looming problems of growth. The leading theory of the cause of erosion is the "Greenhouse Effect" whereby carbon monoxide exhaled by industrialized civilization retains the earth's temperature which melts the polar icecaps causing the oceans to rise about an inch every decade. Gradually the swelling water washes away at the shorelines, and storms and currents take their toll as well. Ecological experts — there are hosts of them in East Coast Universities, such as Duke and Florida — have argued for years that it is folly to live on a barrier island, because inevitably it will be submerged. Whatever the cause of the phenomenon, it has been going on at least since the Spanish were here; the ruins of a villa have been reported sitting on the ocean floor a few hundred feet off the north end.

In the early days the general attitude on the Island about beach erosion was that the problem belonged to the people who owned property on the oceanfront, and it was up to them to cope with it. They built seawalls to hold off the battering of the sea and groins to contain the sand washed laterally by the currents. The seawalls suffered, crumbling at their bases, the earth behind them sagging, but with constant repair they helped stave off the sea and still do. The groins proved useless.

By 1972, the fact had begun to dawn on the residents that erosion had become a threat — a distant one, to be sure — to the whole Island, and that it was everybody's concern. The Town government stepped in, and after meeting with the engineers and studying their projections, it decided that the best way to fight erosion was to build up the beach itself. Beach Renourishment became a new phrase in the Islander's lexicon.

Small-scale renourishment had been tried in the fifties and continued intermittently until 1970. Sand was dredged from the Intracoastal and dumped on the beach by truck. Experts keeping track of this prolonged operation made the discouraging notation: "...1,500,000 cubic yards of sand placed ...2,500,000 yards lost due to normal erosion." In 1972 the Town, now fully in charge, hauled and dumped 2,800,000 more cubic yards; no headway. "So," said Town Manager Vande Weghe, "we decided to go big and stop fooling around with these little projects." From then on sand was pumped

engine, a police car, paid a Martin County Deputy Sheriff and a policeman to patrol the place and kept in touch with Stuart on administrative matters. But it did not have the authority to accomplish the new objectives. Nor could — or would — the County grant the authority as long as Jupiter Island remained an unincorporated entity. "The time had come," recalls Permelia Reed, "to incorporate," to create a new town. Self-rule was the answer.

Mrs. Reed led the delegation of residents to the Stuart Courthouse where the Commissioners sat. The ensuing meeting was amiable; "They were very nice about it," says Mrs. Reed, "they weren't against it." The delegation returned satisfied, and the Town of Jupiter Island came into being May 11, 1953. On that historic day in the Murphy Building, a wartime barracks J.V.R. had brought over from Camp Murphy and set up on Riverside Road, the first town meeting assembled and appointed the first five Town Commissioners who in turn elected the first Mayor and the first Vice Mayor. There were other firsts: an Executive Department, Departments of Finance, Health, Public Works, Fire and Police. Adolf Urfer was appointed Town Clerk and Treasurer; Admiral Richard B. Tuggle became Deputy Town Clerk and Deputy Treasurer, Tax Assessor and Town Manager.

During that same busy year the infant Town built a two-room addition to the firehouse for $4,000, and this annex became the Town Hall. Town Manager Tuggle wrote in his daily log that he had considered — but decided against — filling it with second-hand furniture for only $250. It was replaced in 1972 by a building of quiet presence and charm which was dedicated to Permelia and Joseph Reed "In honor of their leadership and foresight in the creation of this community."

Other Mayors: Robert E. McConnell, 1955-1961 and J. Burr Bartram, 1961-1963 (top), Gordon Lamont, 1967-1977, who served the longest, and Myron A. Wick, Jr., 1977-1983.

onto the beach from a dredge anchored 3,500 feet out. Four times the vast operation took place, the sand and salt water sucked up from the sea bottom by the dredge's pumps pouring beachward in a huge pipe. By August, 1987, 6.1 million cubic yards of sand had enriched the shorefront.

It takes time and patience to measure the effectiveness of the pumpings, and as of this writing the results of the first three (1973, 1978 and 1983) are in. Private engineering firms declared them effective. So, too, did Florida's Department of Natural Resources, an official stamp of approval. The new sand built up the beach 29 feet. Significantly, it also built up the underwater profile, extending a shallower sea bottom farther and farther out with each pumping, thus forcing the waves to break farther and farther out from the shore. After three pumpings at five-year intervals the beach, at the least, held its own; at the most, it gained a little.

The price of renourishment is high, but the alternative is a defenseless island. The four pumpings cost $11 million, more than half the Town's tax revenues for those 14 years or about $1.80 a cubic yard of sand. Money for the first pumping was raised by contributions from residents, resulting in a few paying a lot and some paying nothing. So the Commission enacted an erosion tax to fund the Town's renourishment program that would continue indefinitely. By 1987, all residents were paying 3.7 mills (a mill is one dollar per thousand assessment) which funded the 1987 pumping at a cost of $3 million plus $300,000 to satisfy a new demand — monitoring the turpidity (sand count) in the ocean water for three years after the pumping.

One might ask why the State with a deep concern for its beaches and the tourists they attract does not pay a part of renourishment costs. The fact is that it does pay up to 50 percent, but only if the community provides every quarter of a mile a public access — plus parking area — to the beach that is to be renourished. Thus the Town does not accept state aid.

The pumpings were complicated operations to put together. Town Manager Robert Vande Weghe was the unshakeable force in seeing them through difficulties ranging from equipment failures and bad weather to voluminous governmental red tape which mounted with each pumping. Indeed, the most troublesome part of pumping sand was getting permission to do it. This took an average of half a year plus the efforts of Mr. Wade Hopping, a Tallahassee lawyer who knew his way through the labyrinth. The Department of Environmental Regulation (DER) in Tallahassee is a body of busy environmentalists brimming with the pure ecological doctrines of east coast academia. It is empowered to issue a pumping permit, but it does so only after the Town agrees to stipulations intended to protect the ecology. Thus, inspections of the pumping sites had to be made and pumping schedules agreed to. The DER insisted that off-shore reefs, with the underwater life living on them, be kept free of new sand. This required intricate plots of the sea bottom complicated by allowances for unforseen tide flows and disruptive weather.

But even after the DER finally issues its permit, the permission process still has a long way to go. It must be cleared by everyone else who has a stake in your beach: 14 agencies including the Department of Natural Resources (DNR) in Tallahassee, the Army Corps of Engineers in Jacksonville, and the Fish and Wildlife service of the Department of the Interior in Washington, D.C., all focusing their massive attention on the issuance of three permits. Each has its own demands to make, adding round after round of meetings and voluminous exchanges of letters filled with new stipulations and cancellations of old ones. For example, in 1987, the nesting time of the sea turtles presented an unexpected complication.

Turtles are blessed with the permit protection of not one but two environmental sub-agencies within two larger ones. When they are in the ocean the turtles belong to one such sub-agency which has permit-okay power. Once they flipper their way onto the beach they and their eggs and their hatched offspring fall under the jurisdiction of another with similar power. To make matters worse, the Fish and Wildlife Service suddenly limited the size of the areas to be renourished, and it did this to be sure that the new sand did not block the turtles' way up the beach. — a distant possibility that had not worried the bureau in the past. Requests for a mile of pumping coverage were cut in half, stringent time limits were set which, should a rough surf develop (which it did), would be impossible to meet. As stipulation kept pouring into Town Hall from Tallahassee, it occurred to the Commissioners that given a choice between people and turtles, people didn't have a chance.

The Greenhouse Effect reminds us that the ocean is rising an inch a decade, a rate of submersion whose end, whatever that may turn out to be, is an eternity away. It is the storm that howls in from the sea that wreaks the immediate, shocking damage: six feet of newly pumped-in beach gouged out overnight; the upper North end flooded and homes tilting crazily; Beach Road threatened at its foundation. Back in the fifties the inroads of the advancing sea and one of Permelia Reed's most ingenious accomplishments came together in a unique situation.

Waves pounding over an eroded portion of beach were undermining a stretch at the South end of Beach Road which was then A1A, a north-south thoroughfare. The traffic on this road was frequent, noisy, worrisome, and Permelia came up with a deft plan to put a stop to it: persuade the County to exchange the designation A1A with 707 on the mainland and thus divert the rumble of trucks and cars from the Island. In her book "Kaleiodoscope of Jupiter Island from the year 1931", she wrote: "The struggle over having State Road A1A removed to the mainland and replaced by State Road 707 took place in 1952. The residents at that time were paying more than one third of the county taxes so our appeal in person to the county commissioners had some substance. Dr. St. John, Gene Tunney and J.V.R. were the main speakers, but the residents turned out to a man in the old rather small, airless courthouse and were heard favorably by the commissioners."

In the meantime the new 707 was now in imminent danger; obviously it would have to be moved. A debate began among the residents over how far west it should be routed, and it went on at length while the sea beat away at the roadbed. One group, which included Robert McConnell and George W. Merck, wanted it moved considerably farther inland than the other which included the Reeds. "Too much land would

have been lost," recalls Mrs. Reed. The State, exasperated by the argument and the delay, proclaimed a deadline. Then a storm rose out of the northeast and just about finished off the road. In the urgency of a quick decision the Reed plan won the day, and the famous "S Curve" was created. Merck philosophized in a letter dated 1954: "My concern is that I and my neighbors had not put in the road ourselves where we wanted it originally. If it hadn't been for the storm which cut the old road and forced immediate action by the state road authorities, I am sure we would have gotten around to it in time."

The forecasts of sociologists that there would be a U.S. population shift to the warm-climate belt is coming to pass with frightening accuracy. California is now the country's most populated state with Texas in second place and Florida close on the heels of Pennsylvania for third. Achieving the top rung is a dubious honor, but Florida likes to tout it. Aside from the tourists streaming in and out, 900 people pour into this state every day to stay. The Town population has not grown in proportion, but it has increased enough (140 residents in 1953 to 1600 today) to raise concerns that the quality of life here could suffer the fate that always seems to come when too many people crowd into one choice spot.

The price of real estate has soared into its own stratosphere, but that has not deterred the buyers. A small new house with swimming pool on a 100 by 150 foot lot (close to

The Town staff: (front row, left to right) Police and Fire Chief, Jack Curry; Elizabeth Chartier, secretary-bookkeeper; Gloria Schaus, Town Clerk; Jimmy Graham, head of the sanitation department;

Lieutenant, Jim Spurgeon. Back row: Town Managers, Bob Vande Weghe (left), in office from 1972 through 1987, and Bill Mallery, who has been in office since April 1987.

"When There is a Constabulary Duty to be Done."

Former Town Manager, Bob Vande Weghe, recalls some surprising moments in the enforcement of the law.

Gilbert and Sullivan were right. "A policeman's lot is not a happy one." But it is interesting.

There was the case of the stolen car. One of the residents had a few too many to drink. He was an older man; he had been to the Yacht Club and some of his friends drove him home. He woke up the next morning and didn't see his car in the driveway. So he called the police. Lieutenant Jack Curry went down to see him and said, "Where were you last night?"

"Down at the Yacht Club."

So Jack went to the Yacht Club and sure enough found the car parked there. So he came back and said, "Your car is parked at the Yacht Club."

"Whoever stole the car," said the man, "must have brought it back to the Yacht Club afterwards."

Jack said, "Well, we'll bring it back up to you here, but the car is locked."

Then the man said, "Well, I guess he took the keys with him."

Jack said, "Could we check the pockets in the coat you wore last night?"

The resident said, "Sure." So he checked the pockets and found the keys. And now for the mystery. "I can understand stealing the car and bringing it back," the man said, "but how did he get the keys back in my pocket?"

A man named Klibens called the police three nights in a row, complaining about prowlers walking around his house shining a light in his windows. The police found nothing. On the third night, we stationed a person outside the house to stalk the prowlers. Klibens was in his bedroom. About 11:00 at night he came running out of the house.

"Did you see him?" he asked.

The policeman hadn't seen him. He checked. Nothing. He went inside and sat with Klibens. Sure enough, lights came on outside, reflecting back and forth, shining in the window, and the policeman swore there were prowlers out there. They were fireflies!

One morning I got a call from Permelia Reed.

She said, "Dear Boy, you must do something to stop Ad Holton from shooting owls."

I asked Mrs. Reed where she heard about it.

She said she got it from Betty Kirby. "If you talk to her, she'll tell you all about it."

So I called up Betty Kirby. And she said, "Oh yes. He's been shooting owls; I got it from Bea Miller."

So I called up Bea Miller, and she said, "Oh, yes, he has been shooting owls; he told it himself at a cocktail party. He said that his yard man shot an owl, and it fell into Carter Nichols' yard, and his yard man buried it."

So I then called up Carter Nichols and he said, "Gee, I don't know anything about it. My yard man is outside. Let me call him in."

The yard man said, "No, sir, Mr. Vande Weghe, I never heard anything about this. I never buried an owl in my yard."

Well, Ad Holton at this point was sick and I didn't want to bother him, so I took the bull by the horns and went down to see his yard man.

The yard man said, "No, sir, Mr. Vande Weghe, I never shot any owl. Mr. Holton was bothered by them. They were keeping him awake at night, and he said to go out and shoot them, so I went out and shot up in the air, and the owl flew away. When I came back inside, Mr. Holton said, 'Did you shoot the owl?' And I said, 'Yessir.' He said, 'Let me see it,' and I said, 'I can't, because it fell over next door in Mr. Nichols' yard, and Mr. Nichols' man buried it.'"

the Jupiter Island Club but not on the ocean or waterway) would have gone for around $225,000 ten years ago, but in 1987 it sold for $950,000. Tempted by these prices and concerned by the corresponding rise in property taxes, residents with land to spare have put portions of it up for sale. All the Town can do about this cycle of growth is to control and enforce its present zoning regulations. Lately some form of "up-zoning" has been the talk at dinner parties and Town meetings. A study already made shows that if two acres were required for all further building permits, the construction of 60 to 70 new homes would be prohibited.

Looking back on those eventful years as Mayor, one recalls presiding over some stormy Town Meetings when Permelia was on the warpath. She spoke her mind with devastating critical clarity, and the Mayor struggled to keep his cool and get the best job done. The Town Government and the Hobe Sound Company, which is synonomous with the interests of the Reed family, are the two strongholds of power on the Island. Occasionally, they collided. But they completed many projects jointly and coordinated on many more. Whenever possible, the Reeds attended Town Meetings and took their seats usually on the far right of the first row; Nathaniel a tall, lanky man clutching a yellow pad scribbled with notes, his mother short, erect and proud of bearing as she addressed an attentive Commission. Nathaniel served twice as a Commissioner; his father, once.

The mission of the Town government is to keep the Island and its quality of life flourishing. For the Commission, the Board of Adjustment and the residents too, the times will be more demanding in coming years — more difficult and probably more costly. There are no signs that the bureaucracies will ease the tight band of stipulations for sand pumping permits. To the contrary, they are likely to yank it in a few notches. As for growth, the measures that might be taken to limit it could rile up antagonisms or even legal action. The concluding lines of a judge's decision written in 1961 are most pertinent now. In the Circuit Court of Martin County Judge Williams Sample ruled against two Island residents who challenged the Town's zoning ordinance requiring single-family dwellings as being unreasonable and invalid. The Judge wrote:

"The Community is unique — it is the one and only, different from all others having no like or equal. It is unusual, extraordinary and rare. It was cut from one mold and its counterpart cannot be found elsewhere. Many people would consider it dead — but it is very much alive with genteel living, friendship and compatability. The Town doesn't want what many others have, but many others would be better off if they had more of what this Town has and wants to keep — seclusion, solitude and tranquility."

Crumbling seawalls (left), displaced sand bags, and broken groins have helped save some houses over the years but not the beach.

Eroding bank of sand below Beach Club Snack Bar dramatizes the effects of rising seas and disappearing sand, which must be replaced.

Barge offshore sucks up sand and sends it 3,500 feet through the curving white pipeline to beach. Since 1973, four pumpings have deposited 6.1 million cubic yards at a cost of $11 million.

On shore, sand from the pumping barge spumes out of the pipe under supervision of foreman. Bulldozer smoothes it into place. Preparing for a renourishment is a long, redtape-clogged process requiring three permits from 14 state and federal agencies.

Golf Course — Beautiful,

Bewitching.

The moods of its beauty change as the day passes. The early morning mist leaves a sheen of silver on the grass. At noon the light is high and brilliant; the shadows gather under the trees. But as the sun descends in the west, the shadows lengthen and the light, warmed in gold, streams across the 11th fairway paralleling the Intracoastal, and sparkles on the pond.

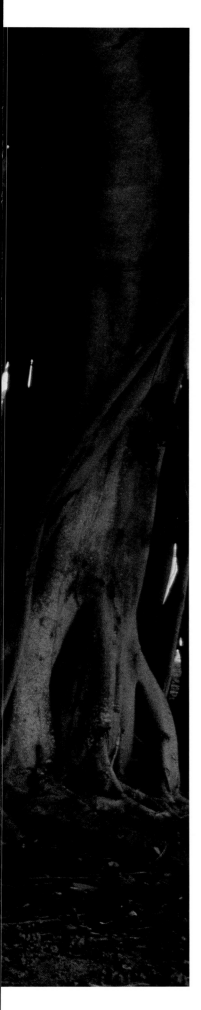

With giant trunk and luxuriant canopy this banyan tree (left), one of the finest on the Island, is a course landmark. So, too, is the Traphagen house (top), built in the 1920s in the Spanish style. The number of errant slice shots that have dropped on its front lawn over the decades is incalculable. The palm trees, stately Jamaican tall, survive as a result of regular treatment against lethal yellowing which has wiped them out in Jamaica and most of South Florida. The 17th hole (above) invites a brave shot over the water.

Water is a hazard on no less than ten holes! In the view (top) it separates the 16th green and the fourth fairway. The view down the seventh fairway (top right) with long shadows of the casuarinas sweeping across it, illustrates Richard Webel's concept that a golf hole should appear pictorially "balanced" and "have an end", in this case a cluster of palms. To the west beyond the 12th green where a golfer makes his putt, lies the Intracoastal and the Hobe Sound shore. The view at right extends across a pond to the 11th fairway which skirts the water's edge.

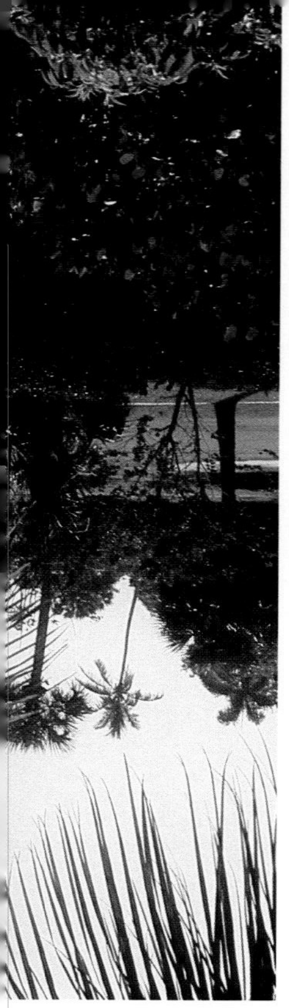

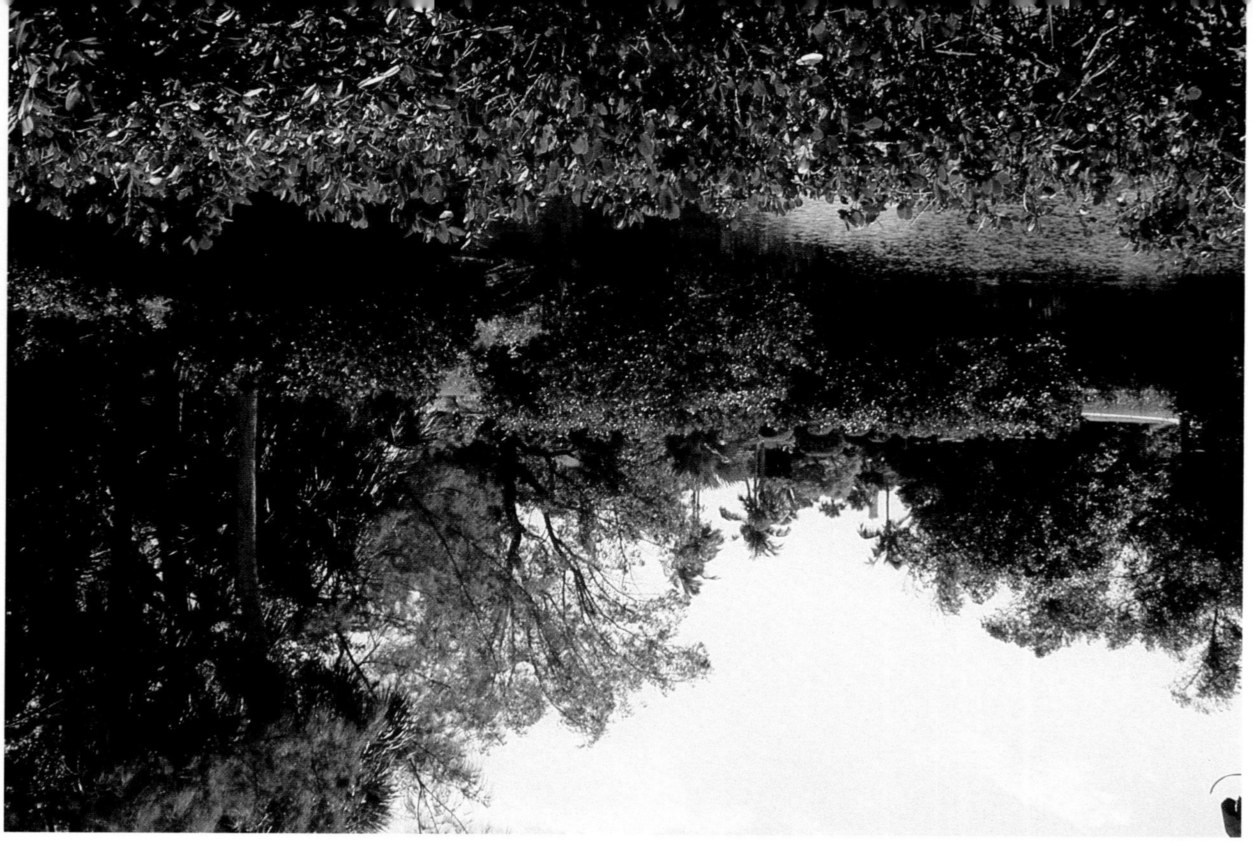

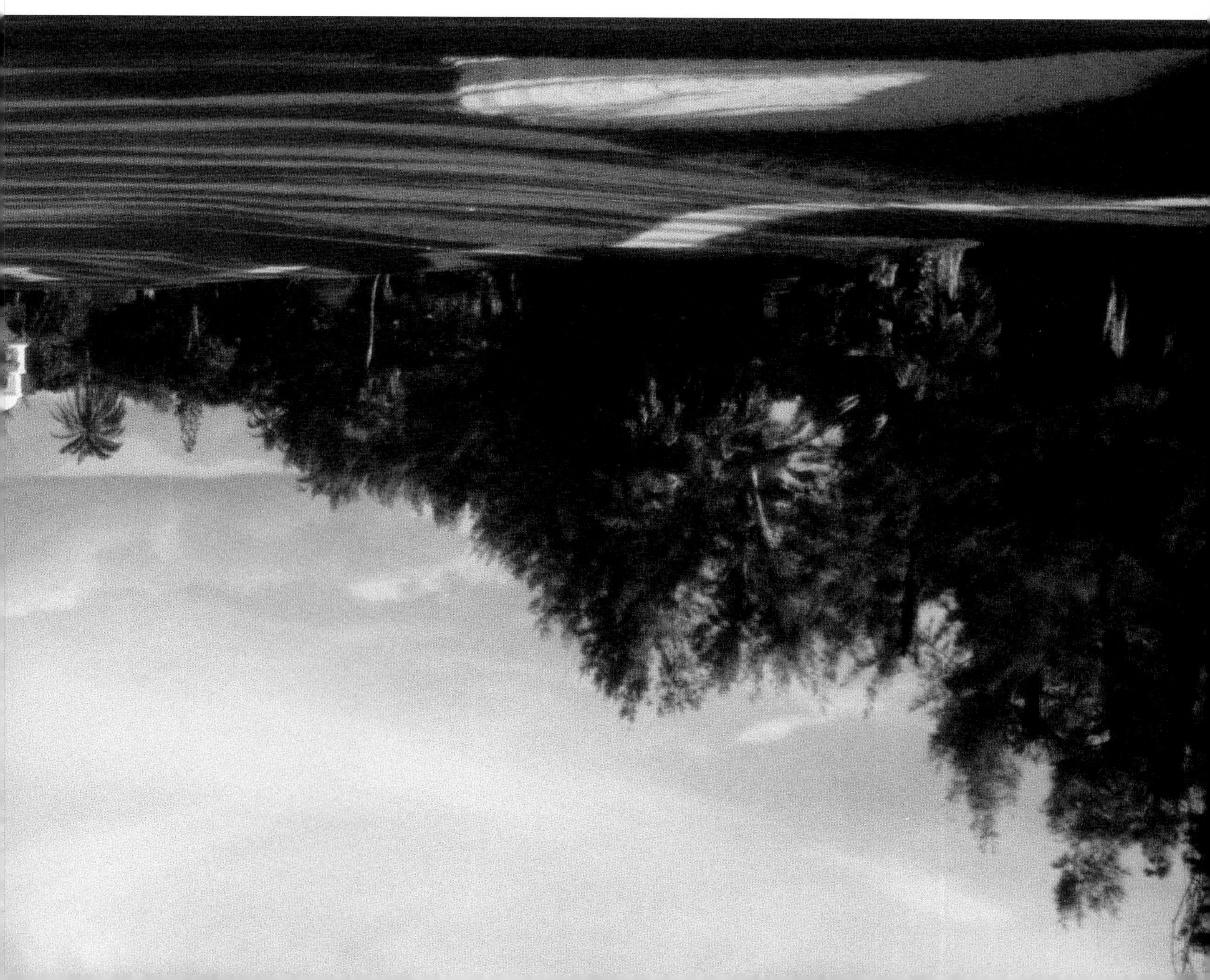

Christ Memorial Chapel is framed by the casuarinas lining the seventh fairway. In 1920, when the casuarinas were but saplings, a fairway running north-south lay to the east inside the dune line and another to the west between Gomez and Links Roads. In the mid-1920s it was decided that these portions of land could be put to use more profitably as building sites. So the golf course was redesigned. The seventh and eighth holes are the only survivors of the original course (see text p. 104).

The two smaller photographs show ponds bordered by fairways and kept stocked with fish by Stuyvesant Pierrepont who catches the fish in the waterway or elsewhere and brings them here. Bass and bluegill share the pond at left: two others (far left) have tarpon and snook. (Golfballs also find their way into them in large numbers.) Many varieties of waterfowl inhabit the ponds, and swans have recently joined them.

103

Pretty Pictures, But Golfer Beware!

by Cecil McIver

To an experienced golfer the course at first glance looks innocent and inviting. No unusual hazards leap to the eye, no long carries over water or across long stretches of sand. He looks at the score card and finds that the course is relatively short. It is 375 yards shorter than Seminole, 421 yards shorter than Jupiter Hills, two famous, difficult courses nearby.

Not until he has played Jupiter Island a few times does a golfer begin to respect it and to be somewhat baffled by it. He may find the first nine easy, but if he is a long hitter he may also find that there isn't much margin for error. Fairways are narrow, closely flanked by casuarinas or dense jungle. More often than on other courses he has played, his drives are out of bounds or in trouble. By the end of the round it is likely that somewhere he has met with disaster — sand, water, a tangle of mangrove.

Many golfers who are proud of their low handicaps have found that, day-in, day-out, their scores are higher here than at Seminole, which is always listed among the world's ten most celebrated courses. They don't like to admit, even to themselves, that this "little" Jupiter Island course is more than they bargained for — they just had an off day. But giving good golfers such off days seems to be its bewitching habit.

One fine golfer, familiar with many courses, says that this one is the most unforgiving he has ever encountered. He is William Battle, an Island resident and President of the United States Golf Association. Battle hits a long ball and carries a four handicap at Seminole, a six at Jupiter Island, and he attributes the differences to the greater demand for accuracy off the tee. On most other courses the fairways are more generous, and the golfer can spray a drive and still recover. Not so here. "There are no weak holes on this course," Battle says. He also regards the beautiful 14th as "one of the best par threes around. Oliver Havens, also an Island resident and until recently the General Counsel for the U.S.G.A., plays here and at Seminole, and he finds that this shorter course can be very demanding. He senses that he swings more freely on Seminole's more generous fairways. His scores there are more consistent. He makes both higher and lower scores here, but his average on both courses is about the same. So the hazards of the "little" course can be psychological as well as physical.

Paradoxically, this "little" course appears to be less difficult for the higher handicapped player who is not tempted to whale the ball for long distances. It dares the compulsive long hitter to go all out and lures him into overlooking or underestimating the hazards lying in ambush. It is always possible for a golfer to master this course by playing it safe — keeping his driver in the bag and using irons mostly. It is *possible*, but it is against a true golfer's nature, and the "little" course knows it.

The way this beautiful and treacherous creature came into being was a rather hit or miss phenomenon. The first golf course on Jupiter Island was built by the Land Mortgage Co. of Yorkshire, England, under the supervision of William Angas. It was a part of the resort envisioned by the British speculators, a nine-hole course that was completed by 1922.

The first tee was in the neighborhood of the present golf house. The green was some 370 yards due east between Beach Road, then a dirt track, and the sand dunes bordering the beach which was very broad, even at high tide.

This little blue heron (above) is a familiar sight on the pond near the practice putting green. Red, white and pink night-blooming water lilies and multi-colored day bloomers make the pond a palette of bright color. Gil Cavanaugh (right) has been the Club Professional for 35 years, only the second in the Club's history! Teatime every afternoon brings together golfers, tennis players, bridge players and young children, at the golfhouse (below).

GIL CAVANAUGH
GOLF PROFESSIONAL

DWIGHT CAMPBELL

MAX MINNICK

DONALD
VANAUGH

The second and third holes ran northward between the dune line and Beach Road. The fourth and fifth holes doubled back; the sixth and seventh holes turned north again between Gomez Road and Links Road. The eighth and ninth holes ran back towards the first tee on the west side of Links Road. Although there were few houses on the Island then, there were enough golfers around to justify the hiring in 1922 of George Blagg as the first teaching pro. He was destined to remain with the Club until 1952 and enjoy his retirement until he passed away, at age 100, in 1986 in West Palm Beach.

In 1923 the Olympia Improvement Corp., having bought out the British, set up plans for an extensive housing development along the beach front, a more lucrative use of the real estate than the game of golf. So the golf course was moved slightly westward, and it survives today as the first nine holes of the present course. During the move only the fourth and fifth holes — now the seventh and eighth — remained the same. The fairways were grassy but full of burrs, and the "greens" were circular patches of sand. There was no clubhouse; the pro shop occupied a corner of the tennis shop. However, the process of improvement which has continued for more than 60 years had begun.

When J.D. Bassett and his family came to Jupiter Island in 1925 and built their homes near the sixth tee, the greens had been planted with rye grass and water piped to each green at which a faucet and a hose were provided. Jim Black's father was hired to water the greens every evening, and he did this traveling from one green to the next by mule.

In 1933 the Hobe Sound Company took over the Island, and a year later the Army Corps of Engineers began construction of the Intracoastal Waterway from Peck's Lake to Hobe Sound. From the Army engineers Joseph Reed obtained thousands of yards of sand to fill the swamp which then occupied the western half of the Island. This would make possible the later expansion of the golf course to 18 holes.

In 1953 Gil Cavanaugh took the job of Club Pro. In 1954 Permelia Reed asked the eminent landscape architect, Richard Webel, to design a golf house. Having completed that commission, Webel turned his attention to the expansion of the golf course itself. He had experience working on the course at the Greenbrier and had definite views about what he wanted to accomplish. "When you look down a fairway it should be a picture — when landscaping I am really always making pictures — and it should be both beautiful and balanced. And it should have an end."

The land to the west of the two fairways, which had been partially filled in 1934, had grown into a forest of Australian pines. The trees were felled and burned. More fill was obtained by dredging two ponds adjacent to the first two fairways, and the present 10th, 11th, 12th, 17th and 18th holes were created. Riverview Drive was also made at this time.

It was now 1957 and two years later Nathaniel Reed returned from military service in 1959. "It was obvious," says Nat, "that the Island residents really wanted an 18-hole golf course and not the eclectic 14-hole golf course Mother was determined they were going to have. The only place to expand was across to Fullman Island. Luckily the Corps of Engineers began to dredge the Intracoastal Waterway again, and this gave us a rare opportunity to obtain the fill we needed. The Island residents advanced the money to the Company to build the four holes and Dick Webel laid out a plan — a gorgeous plan — for the 13th, 14th, 15th and 16th holes. The land was cleared by bulldozer and everything was burned in

preparation for the dredging to come. Only the black mangrove trees on the left side of the 16th fairway were untouched. Captain Milling was the dredging contractor — a real character — and I can remember Dick asking: 'Captain Milling, if we leave the pipe down three hours how much fill will we have?' Captain Milling said: 'Well, Mr. Webel, I never thought of that.' Dick, you see, had realized that by putting the fill where he wanted it he would never have to use a bulldozer for grading.

"On the Monday morning that work started, Mr. Murphy, the land contractor, arrived with several tractors to do the grading, and Permelia, Nat and Dick, all in hard hats, were waiting for him. 'I am not going to need any tractors,' Dick said. 'Why not?' Murphy asked. 'Because I am going to use the dredge, and with the fill I am going to build all the high points for the trees and greens and let the land find its own level. I'll build the land so that it has natural grading and drainage.' And that is how it turned out: no bulldozers needed. But it wasn't as easy as it sounded.

"We got a trailer out onto Fullman Island," Nat recalls, "and I lived in the trailer for the four or five weeks that the dredging took. We put in stakes to mark the elevations we wanted, and when the fill from the dredge reached the right elevation in one place, we added more pipe and began to fill the next area. We had to change the pipe every three hours or so. Mr. Murphy was bitterly disappointed when we sent away his bulldozers, because he was looking forward to moving 100,000 yards of fill at a dollar a yard — but we never had to move one yard.

"There was a lot of wear and tear on me though! I got up at 3 o'clock in the morning to move that damn pipe, and I had to get up again at 6 o'clock and every three hours around the clock! I was dead by the time the thing was done! But it was a great experience. The guys who worked the pipe were a pretty rough lot, but they liked beer, and I figured I could bribe them with cold beer even at 3 o'clock in the morning! To add lengths of pipe you had to stop the dredge, get some men off the barge, haul additional lengths of pipe (which were heavy) and couple them together in such a way that they would fill the next area. Then we would have a couple of beers and send the men back to the barge to get a little more sleep. In another couple of hours I would check the pipes and the elevations, and if another move was necessary I'd holler across to the barge, and out the men would come again. They were pretty nice guys to do that."

With the completion of the last four holes the course had its full eighteen, but improvements continued to be made. In 1963 the 3rd, 4th and 5th holes were redesigned. The 3rd and 17th were redesigned twice, in 1978 and 1987. Eleven greens also were replanted with bent grass in 1987 and several holes modified by changes to tees and bunkers.

The Jupiter Island course is a reflection of Nathaniel Reed's love of the game (he set the Club's amateur record score of 65, or 7 under par) and his insistence in keeping it up to high golf standards. And it also reflects his fascination with nature. During the summers, landscaping teams are busy all around the course. By 1988 more than 250 varieties of shrubs, vines and trees had been planted, giving privacy and individuality to the fairways, enhancing the balanced-picture qualities of Dick Webel's designs. The vistas and intimate views are enlivened with colors that are soft in the mornings and come ablaze when the sun lowers in the west, and the golfer wonders what happened to his game that day.

THE STAFF

EDITOR
George P. Hunt

ASSOCIATE EDITOR
Hobart Lewis

ART DIRECTOR
James N. Baker

ASSISTANT ART DIRECTORS
Pete Richardson, Rose Hidalgo, Kellie Knight-Jocoy

DIRECTOR OF PHOTOGRAPHY
Bridg Griswold

DIRECTOR OF RESEARCH
Pauline B. Nutting

ASSISTANT DIRECTOR OF RESEARCH
Constance L. Bell

AUTHORS
Colt Adams, Billie Agnew, Colby Chester
Sallie Caler, Tom Green, Hobart Lewis
Norah Lind, Cecil McIver, John Mulliken
Sealy Newell, Nathaniel Reed, Tom Stanley
Seymour St. John

INTERVIEWEES
Mr. & Mrs. James Black, Arthur Broderick,
Mr. & Mrs. Kemp Caler, Gilbert Cavanaugh,
Mrs. Hugh Chatham, Jack Curry, Mr. & Mrs. William Deaton,
Mrs. James Diamond, John Duberg, Mrs. Morris R. Eddy,
Thomas Fair, Eugene Ferguson, Frederick Gordon,
Edward H. Hamm, Mrs. Truman M. Hobbs,
Mrs. Solon C. Kelley, Jr., Mrs. Kathryn B. Leisy,
Thomas M. Lind, Mrs. Pauline McArthur, Mrs. Nelson S. Mead,
Mrs. John H. Mulliken, Jr., Mrs. Philip E. Nuttle, James Pressly,
Adrian P. Reed, Mrs. Joseph V. Reed, Nathaniel P. Reed,
Mrs. John Robinson, Thomas B. Stanley, Jr., Rev. Seymour St.
John, Donald St. Onge, Admiral Richard B. Tuggle,
Mrs. Dolly Wickwire Urban, Robert Vande Weghe,
Richard K. Webel, Harold White, Roebuck Williams

PUBLISHING STAFF
Mrs. Bernhard M. Auer, John Granberg,
Mrs. C.E. Bayliss Griggs, Mrs. George P. Hunt,
Mrs. Janice King, Mrs. Hobart Lewis, Mrs. Alfred J. Seaman,
Mrs. Joanne Talley

BOOK COMMITTEE
Mrs. Theodore Greef, (Chairwoman), Mrs. Robert M. Blake,
Mrs. Kemp Caler, Mrs. David McElroy, Mrs. G. Sealy Newell,
Mrs. Philip E. Nuttle, Mrs. George W. Offutt, III,
Mrs. Thomas B. Stanley, Jr., Mrs. E. Carroll Stollenwerck

TREASURER
Mrs. A.L. Cole

PUBLISHER
Bernhard M. Auer

PHOTO CREDITS
Page 4-5: Suzanne J. Engelmann (1983 Photo)
Page 6-7: Bridg Griswold
Page 8: Suzanne J. Engelmann
Page 9-13: Bridg Griswold
Page 14: Frank Lund & F.P.L. collection
Page 15: Flip Schultze & Frank Lund
Page 16: Bridg Griswold & James N. Baker
Page 17-19: Bridg Griswold
Page 21: Tom Stanley Jr. col.
Page 22: Sam Quincy
Page 25: Jupiter Island Club (JIC) col.
Page 26: Dolly Wickwire Urban col.
Page 29 Top: Seymour St. John col.
Page 29-30: P.P. Reed col.
Page 31: Bridg Griswold & Mrs. S. Kelley col.
Page 32: P.P. Reed col.
Page 33: JIC col.
Page 35: Dolly W. Urban col.
Page 36-37: P.P. Reed col.
Page 40-41: Bridg Griswold & Mrs. J. Diamond col.
Page 42: JIC col.
Page 43: Mrs. J. Diamond col.
Page 44: Donald St. Onge col.
Page 45: P.P. Reed col.
Page 46: Andy Remsen
Page 47: Bridg Griswold
Page 48-49: Bridg Griswold & Mrs. H. Chatham col.
Page 50: Andy Remsen
Page 50-51: Andy Remsen
Page 52-55: Bridg Griswold (except 54 Bottom: Jean Hamm)
Page 56-59: Bridg Griswold & Andy Remsen
Page 60-62: Bridg Griswold
Page 63: Steve Sanacore
Page 64-71: Bridg Griswold & Andy Remsen
Page 72: Sally Newell
Page 74-81: Bridg Griswold
Page 83: Steve Sanacore
Page 85: Dolly W. Urban col.
Page 88-89: Bridg Griswold
Page 90: Town of Jupiter Island col.
Page 91-92: Bridg Griswold
Page 93: Andy Remsen
Page 94: Dulcy Green
Page 95-103: Bridg Griswold
Page 104: Bridg Griswold & James T. Lea
Page 106-107: Andy Remsen

PAPER CREDIT
The fine Ikonorex paper which helped attain the quality printing in this book was the generous gift of Mrs. Beryl Clarke Bridges.

TEXT CREDIT
Description of the view from Jupiter Island lighthouse on page 23 is an excerpt from the book, *Camping and Cruising in Florida,* by James A. Henshall, M.D., 1984

GRAPHICS BY
Commercial Graphic Center, Inc.
Stuart, FL